A-Z ABING

D1766568

CONTENTS

Key to Map Pages   2-3

Map Pages   4-47

Index to Streets, Towns,
Villages, Stations, Hospitals   48-56
& selected Places of Interest

REFERENCE

A Road	**A34**
B Road	**B4017**
Dual Carriageway	
One-way Street	
Traffic flow on A roads is also indicated by a heavy line on the drivers' left.	
Restricted Access	
Pedestrianized Road	
Track / Footpath	
Residential Walkway	
Railway	Heritage Sta. / Tunnel / Station / Level Crossing
Built-up Area	BATH ST.
Local Authority Boundary	
Posttown Boundary	
Postcode Boundary (within Posttown)	
Map Continuation	**10**

Car Park (Selected)	P
Church or Chapel	†
Cycleway (Selected)	☙
Fire Station	■
Hospital	H
House Numbers (A & B Roads only)	218 17
Information Centre	i
National Grid Reference	450
Police Station	▲
Post Office	★
Toilet:	
without facilities for the Disabled	▽
with facilities for the Disabled	▼
Viewpoint	☀
Educational Establishment	
Hospital or Hospice	
Industrial Building	
Leisure or Recreational Facility	
Place of Interest	
Public Building	
Shopping Centre or Market	
Other Selected Buildings	

SCALE

1:15,840   **4 inches to 1 mile**   **6.31 cm to 1 km**   **10.16 cm to 1 mile**

0	¼	½	¾	1 Mile

0	250	500	750	1 Kilometre

Copyright of Geographers' A-Z Map Company Limited

Fairfield Road, Borough Green, Sevenoaks, Kent TN15 8PP
Telephone: 01732 781000 (Enquiries & Trade Sales)
                    01732 783422 (Retail Sales)

www.a-zmaps.co.uk

Copyright © Geographers' A-Z Map Co. Ltd.

Ordnance Survey® This product includes mapping data licensed from Ordnance Survey® with the permission of the Controller of Her Majesty's Stationery Office.

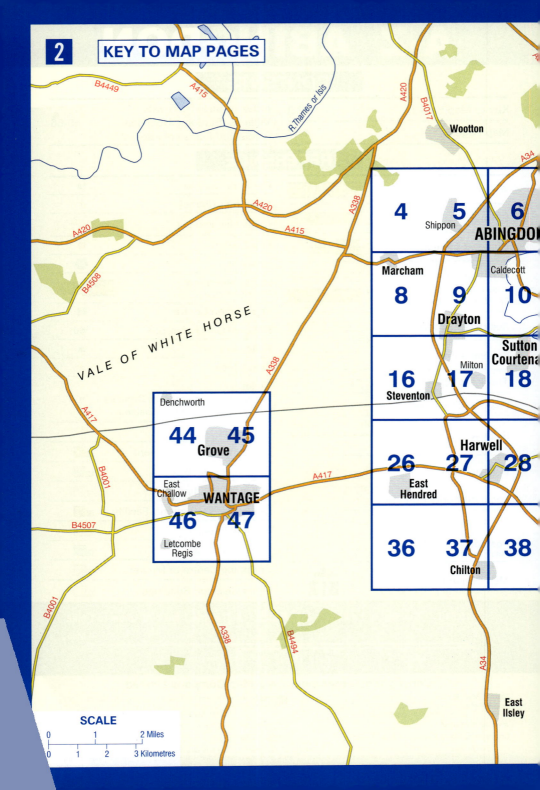

B4449

A415

R.Thames or Isis

A420

B4017

Wootton

A34

A420

A338

A420

A415

4   **5**   **6**

Shippon

ABINGDON

B4508

Caldecott

Marcham

8   **9**   **10**

Drayton

VALE OF WHITE HORSE

A338

Sutton
Courtena

Milton

16   **17**   **18**

Steventon

Denchworth

44   **45**

Grove

A417

Harwell

26   **27**   **28**

East
Hendred

A417

A338

A34

East
Challow

WANTAGE

46   **47**

B4001

B4507

Letcombe
Regis

36   **37**   **38**

Chilton

B4001

A338

B4494

A34

East
Ilsley

SCALE

0   1   2 Miles

0   1   2   3 Kilometres

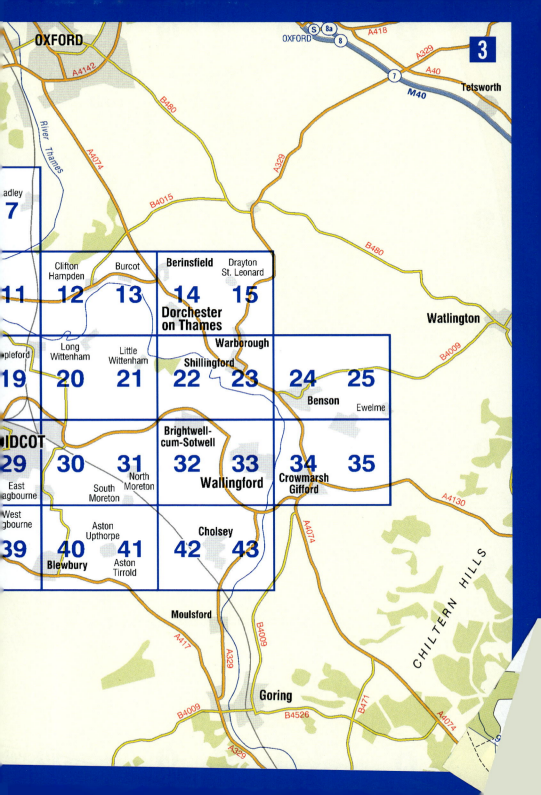

OXFORD

3

OXFORD

Tetsworth

A4142

A418

A329

A40

M40

B480

River Thames

A4074

A329

B4015

adley

7

B480

Clifton Hampden

Burcot

Berinsfield

Drayton St. Leonard

Watlington

11 **12** **13** **14** **15**

Dorchester on Thames

B4009

pleford

Long Wittenham

Little Wittenham

Warborough

Shillingford

19 **20** **21** **22** **23** **24** **25**

Benson

Ewelme

IDCOT

Brightwell-cum-Sotwell

29 **30** **31** **32** **33** **34** **35**

North Moreton

Wallingford

Crowmarsh Gifford

East agbourne

South Moreton

A4130

West gbourne

Aston Upthorpe

Cholsey

A4074

39 **40** **41** **42** **43**

Blewbury

Aston Tirrold

CHILTERN HILLS

Moulsford

A417

A329

B4009

B471

A4074

Goring

B4009

B4526

A329

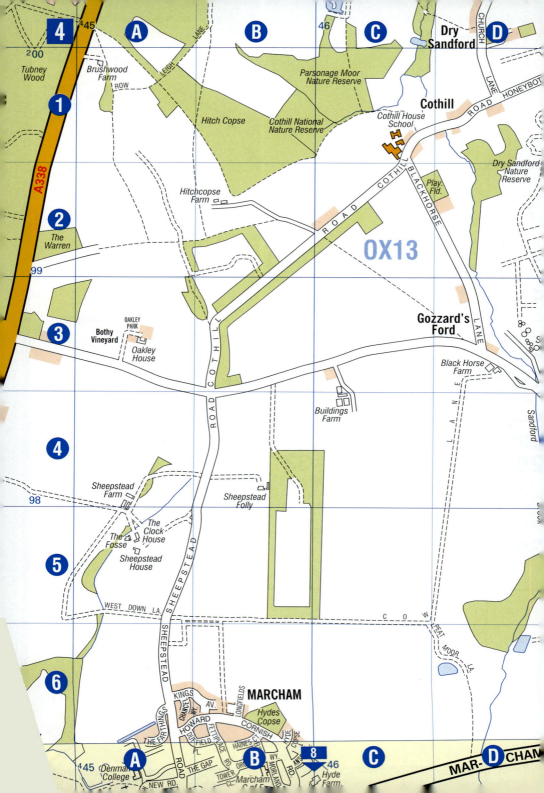

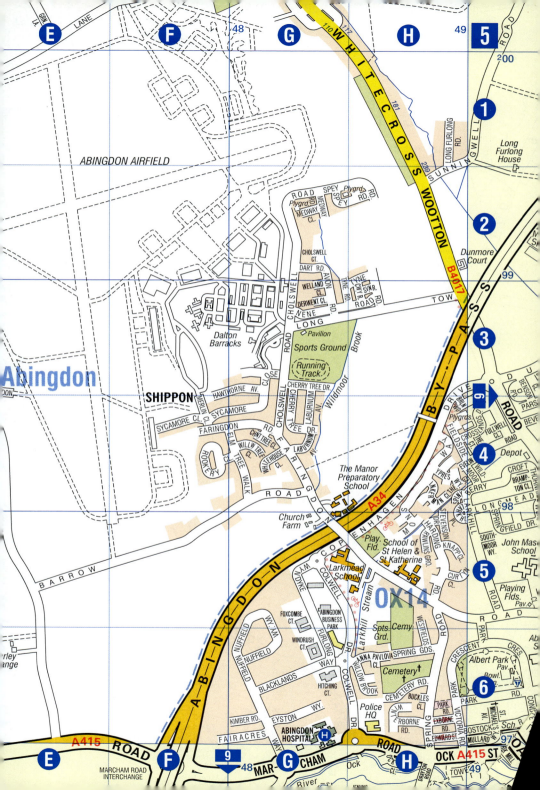

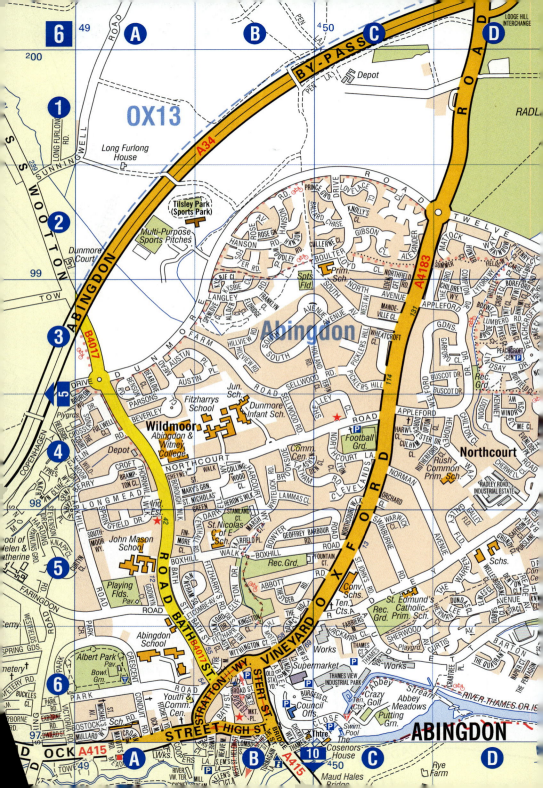

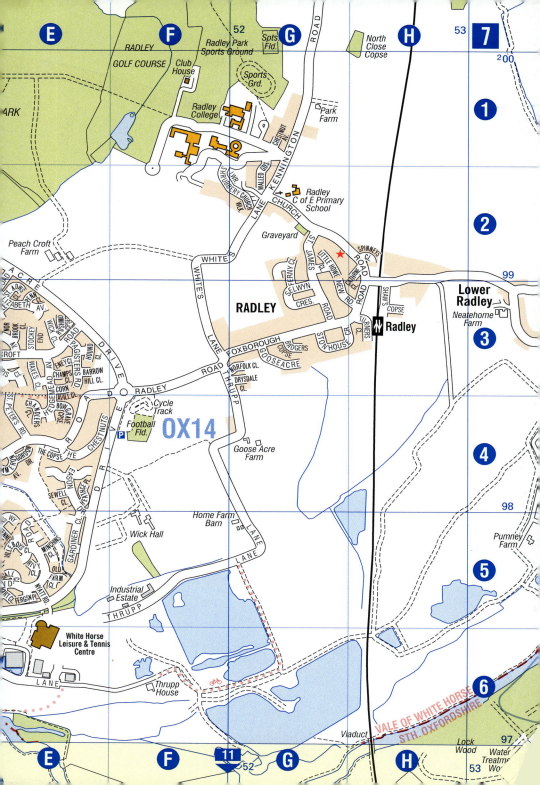

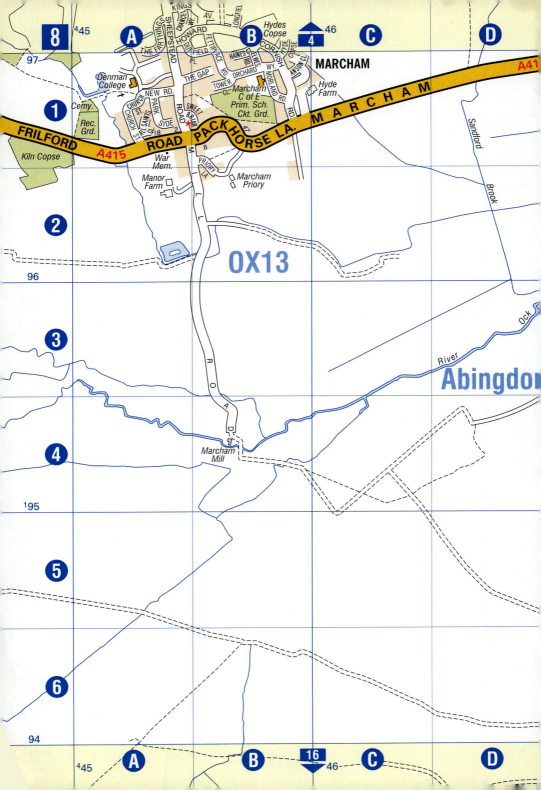

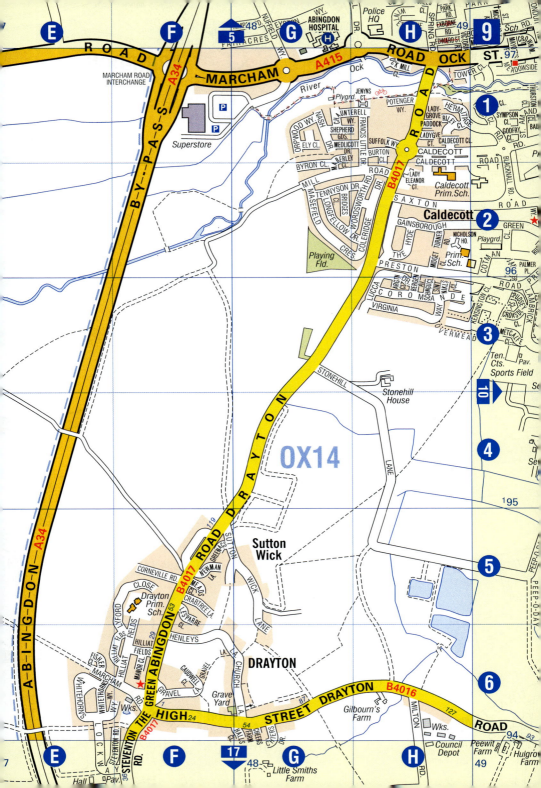

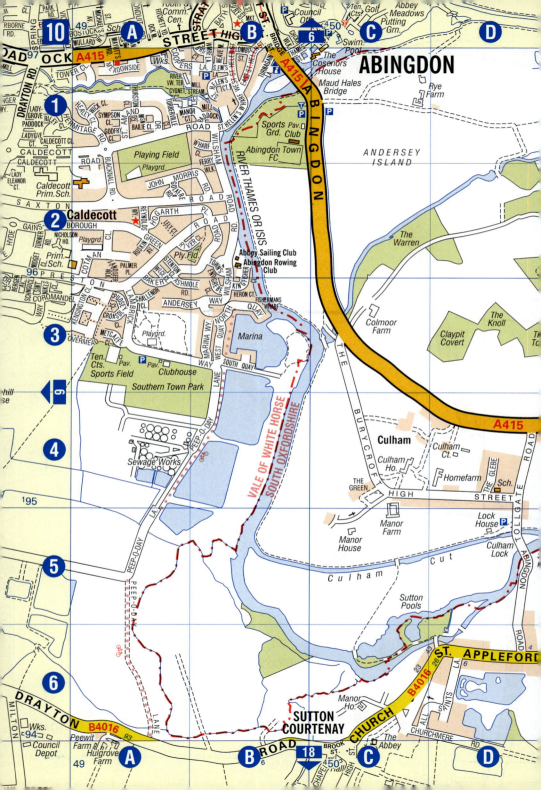

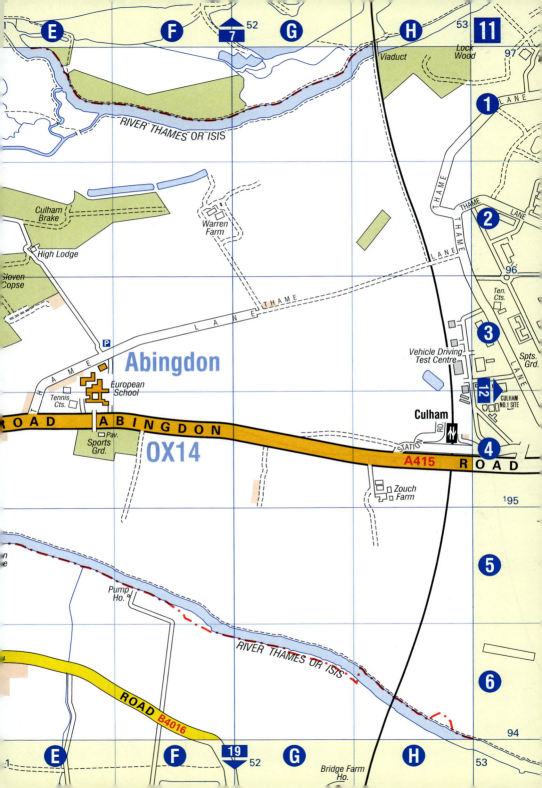

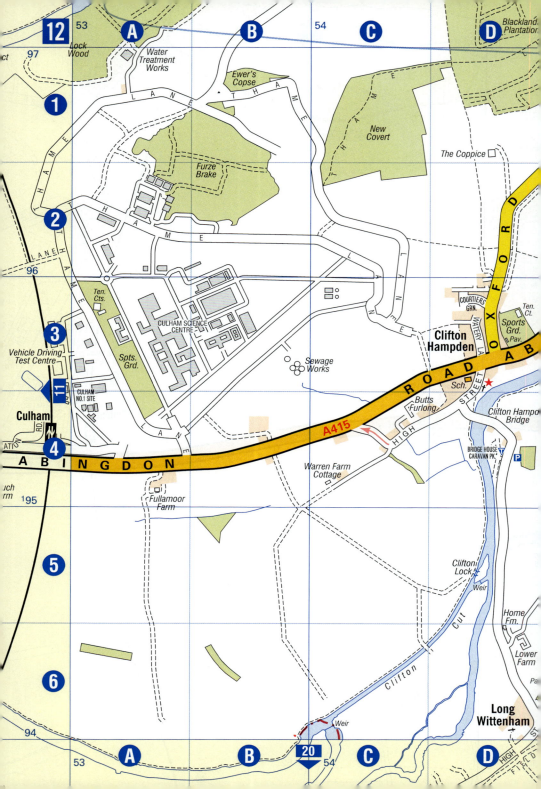

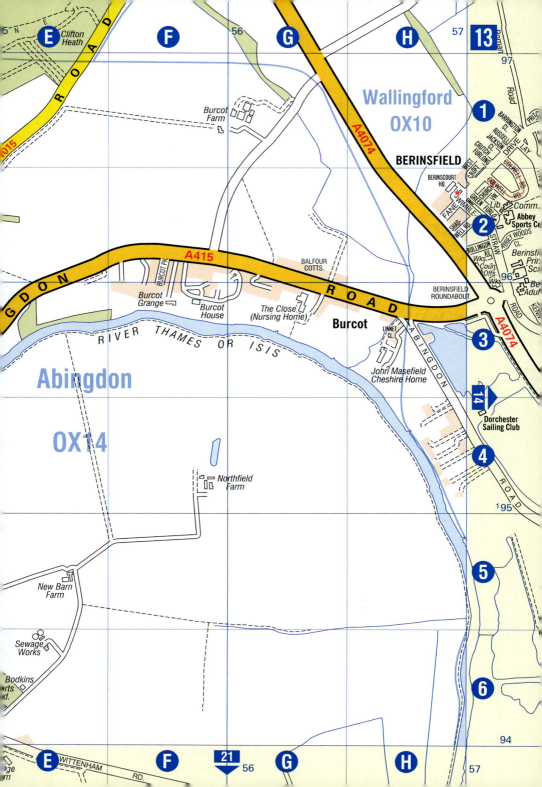

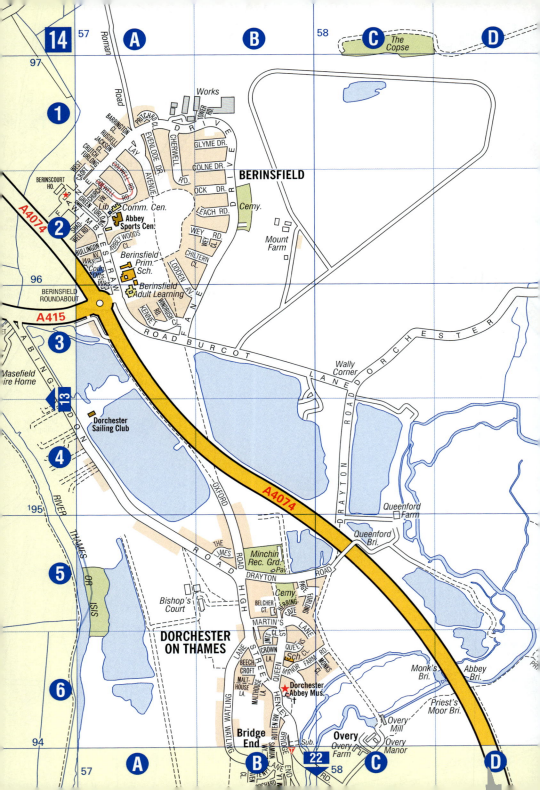

14 57 A B 58 C D

97

C The Copse

1

Works

BARRINGTON
RUSSELL
JACKSON CL.
CRUTCH
FURLONG
WEST CROFT
GREGHURN
GREEN TURN LANE
CHURCH LA.
SHOP
WELL RD.
BULLINGDON
PRITCHARD CL.
LAY
EVENLODE DR.
TOWER RD.
DRIVE
CHERWELL
COLWELL RD.
COLWELL AVENUE

GLYME DR.
COLNE DR.
DOCK DR.
LEACH RD.
WEY RD.
WEY CL.
CHILTERN CL.
LODDEN AV.
WINRUSH CL.
KENNET RD.
DRIVE
FAWLEY
NIMBLESTRAW
ABBEY WOODS CL.

BERINSCOURT HO.

BERINSFIELD

Cemy.

Lib. Comm. Cen.
Abbey Sports Cen.

Berinsfield Prim. Sch.

Berinsfield Adult Learning

Mount Farm

A4074

2

Wks.
Coln.
Ofts.
Wks.

96

BERINSFIELD ROUNDABOUT

A415

3

ROAD BURCOT

Wally Corner

BURCOT LANE

DORCHESTER ROAD

DRAYTON ROAD

Masefield ... re Home

ABINGDON
13

Dorchester Sailing Club

4

A4074

Queenford Farm

Queenford Bri.

195

RIVER THAMES OR ISIS

OXFORD ROAD

THE JAMES ROAD

5

Bishop's Court

HIGH STREET

DRAYTON ROAD

Minchin Rec. Grd.
Pav.

Cemy.

BELCHER CT.
KERRING COTE
PAGE
FURLONG
WORKS
MONKS RD.

DORCHESTER ON THAMES

Monk's Bri.

Abbey Bri.

6

94

MARTIN'S CL.
JAMES CL.
CROWN LA.
BEECH CROFT
MALT-HOUSE LA.
MALTHOUSE LA.
WATLING LANE
WATLING LANE
QUEEN STREET
HENLEY ROAD
BRIDGE END
ROTTEN RW.
SAMIAN WAY
KEBERRY
ORCHARD CL.
LANE END RD.

QUEENS CL.
Sch. CL.
MANOR FARM

★ Dorchester Abbey Mus. †

Bridge End

Sub.

22

57 A B 58 C D

Priest's Moor Bri.

Overy Mill

Overy

Overy Farm

Overy Manor

E **F** ⁴60 **G** **H** **15**

97

Hill Farm
61

Great
Holcombe

HOLCOMBE LA.

Great
Holcombe
Farm

1

Drayton
View

STADHAMPTON RD.

Beauforest
House

Newington
House

Newington

Manor
Farm

**Drayton
St. Leonard**

FORD LANE

THE OSIERS

HIGH ST.

CHURCH LA.

WATER WALK

GRAVEL WALK

Sports
Field

STADHAMPTON RD.

LANE

RIVER THAME

Upper
Grange

2

96

A329

ROAD

Drayton
Ho. Fm.

Heathercombe
Ho.

Ford

3

Wallingford
OX10

Lower
Grange

Lane End
Farm

4

¹95

5

W A Y

W A Y

P A I N

Piggery

MOOR LANE

M E R E

A329

6

MOOR LANE

THAME RD.

Catcharm
Corner

E **F** Court
Farm **23** ⁴60 **G** **H**

LANE

A N E

VW.

94

61

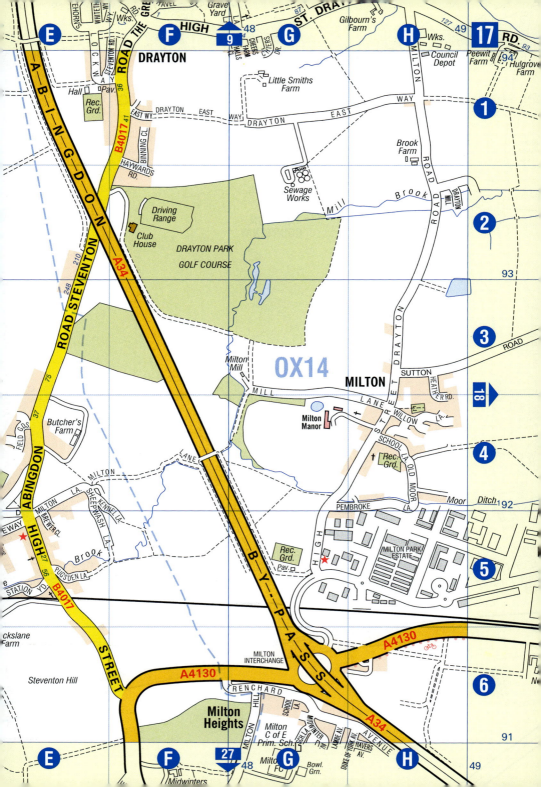

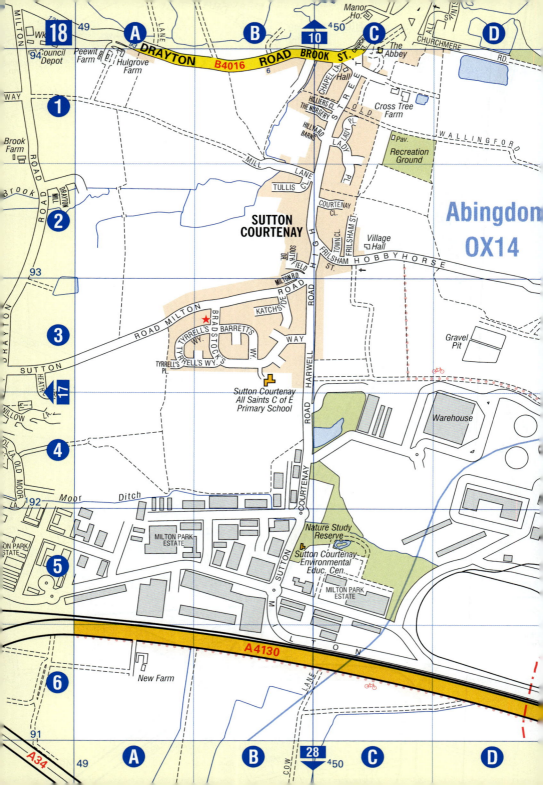

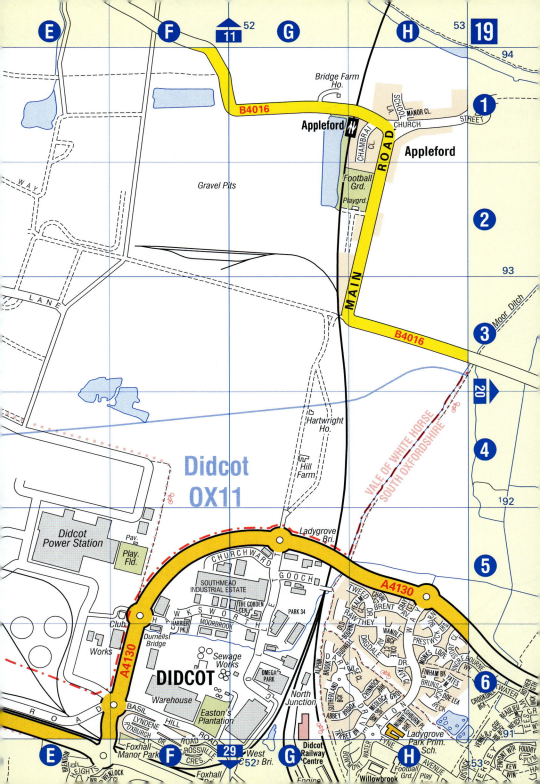

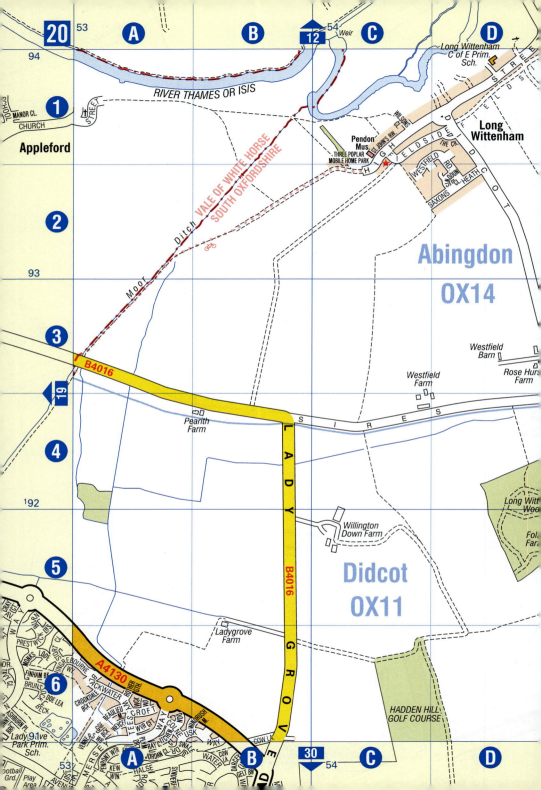

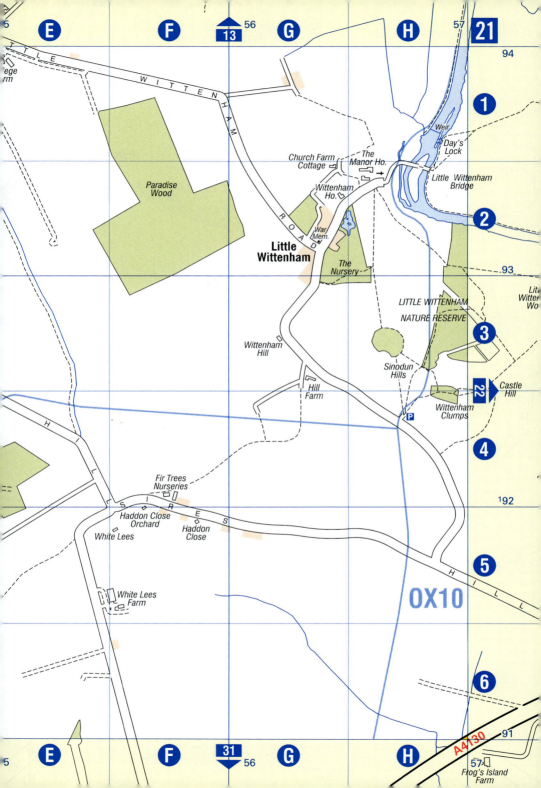

1

LITTLE WITTENHAM ROAD

Paradise Wood

Church Farm Cottage
The Manor Ho.
Wittenham Ho.

Weir
Day's Lock
Little Wittenham Bridge

2

War Mem.

Little Wittenham

The Nursery

93

Lit
Witter
Wo

LITTLE WITTENHAM
NATURE RESERVE

3

Wittenham Hill

Sinodun Hills

Hill Farm

22   Castle Hill

Wittenham Clumps

P

4

¹92

HILL RISE

Fir Trees Nurseries

Haddon Close Orchard
White Lees
Haddon Close

White Lees Farm

HILL

5

OX10

6

A4130

Frog's Island Farm

5

24

61 A B 62 Parsonage Farm C D
94

Lower Berrick Farm

Berrick Salome

WELLER CL.

1

2

Roke

CHAPEL LA.

Roke Farm

93

Rokermarsh

3

Wallingford

23

B4009

ROAD

THE

BRAZE LANE

OX10

Hale Farm

HALE LANE

PORT HILL RD.

SANDS END

THE MEER

BLACKLANDS

WESTFIELD

OPES

NEWTON

GREEN CL.

4

THE CLOSE

SANDS ROAD

RUMBOLDS CL.

ST. ANN'S ROAD

SIDE

WY.

BENSON ROAD

THE CEDARS

STREET

Benson Veteran Cycle Mus.

ESSEY CRES.

Elm Bridge

Hall

192

OXFORD

ELM BRIDGE ROUNDABOUT

Littleworth

LITTLEWORTH RD.

CHURCHFIELD LA.

ROAD B4009

Prim. Sch.

WALLINGTON ROAD

CHILTERN CL.

CROWN

CHAPEL LA.

BUCKN'S CL.

WEST FIELD CL.

WYCHWOOD

OBSERVATORY

OLD BARN CL.

PADDOCK CL.

Control Tower

5

A4074

PENSFIELD

HORSE SHOES LA.

HCC

CASTLE RD.

CHRIST CHURCH RD.

Lib.

CASTLE CL.

CASTLE CT.

HIGH ST.

MORS HILL

College Fm.

STREET

ALDRIDGE CL.

OLD LONDON ROAD

B

R

O

O

K

RIVER THAMES OR ISIS

ST. HELEN'S

GRAVEL HILL

ST. HELEN'S CL.

WAY

COACH WY.

THE MOORLANDS

ST. HELEN'S CRES.

AVENUE

Benson Lock

BENSON

Preston Crowmarsh

91

61 A B 62 Lower Fm. **34** C Bens D

BENS

Hare Hall

Parsons Piece

Scald Hill

Watlington OX49

Rumbold's Copse

2

93

° orks

S A N D S GROVE **B4009** **3** **LANE**

Refuse Tip

LANE

LANE

FIREBRASS HILL

4

¹92

Cottesmore Farm Barns

COTTESMORE

Prospect Farm

Windmill Farm

Hyde Shaw

Fifield Manor

Fifield Farm Barns

EYRES CL.

HIGH

Brownings

GREEN LANE

MARTINS

WINGFIELD CT.

CHAUCER CT.

BRITWELL RD.

HAMPDEN WY.

PARSONS CAT

5

BENSON

EWELME

Grave Yd.

Ewelme Farm

Manor Ho.

Sch.

WINGFIELD CL.

BURROWS

MILL HILL

THE CLOISTERS

The Rectory

The Copper Ho.

6

Play. Fld.

Fords Farm

STREET

Pav. P

Sports Grd.

⁹1

ANDOVER

BELFAST RD.

WORLD WAR WY.

CHIPMUNK WY.

ARGOSY

LANCASTER ROAD

ROAD

JAVELIN WY.

AVENUE

VIKING TER.

MOSQUITO

BLENHEIM

BATTLE

WESSEX

CROSS

BARNETT

DAYS LANE

HENLEY WY.

IRFIELD

Barracks

RAF Benson Prim. Sch.

Rabbits

Cow Common

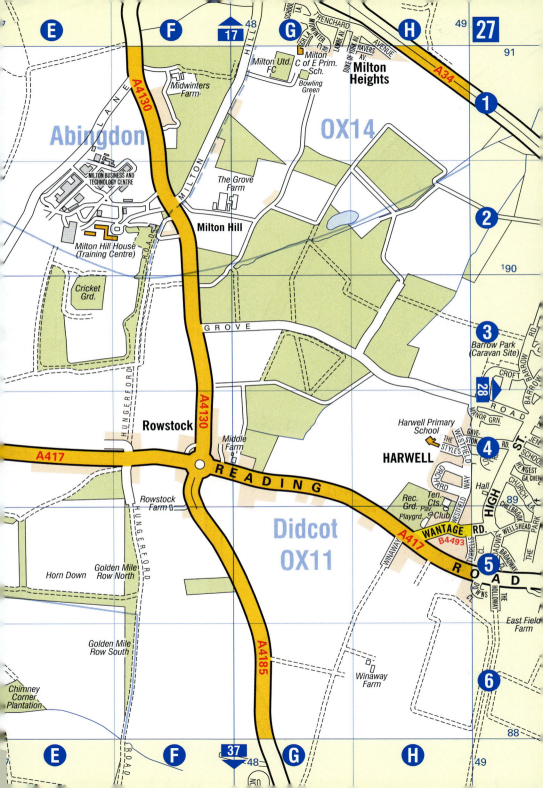

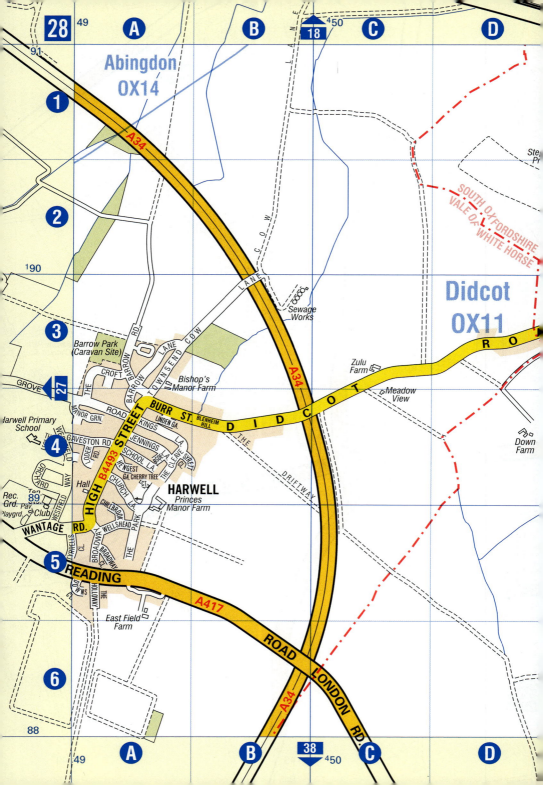

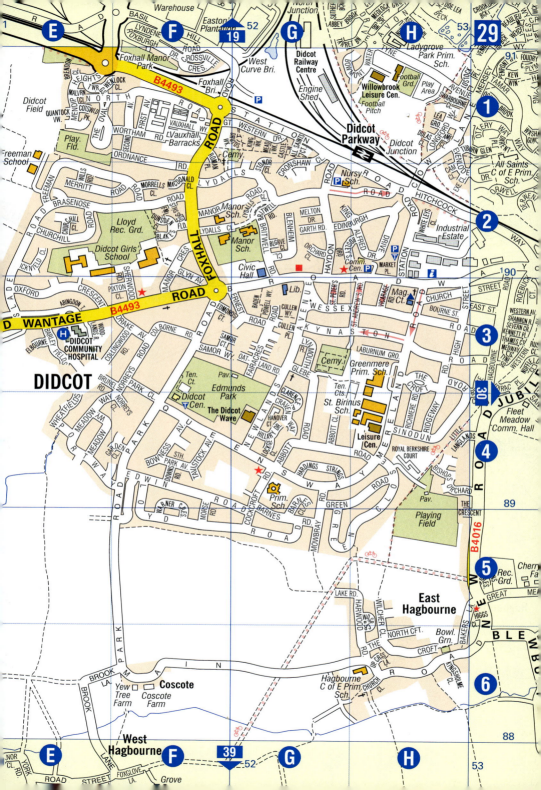

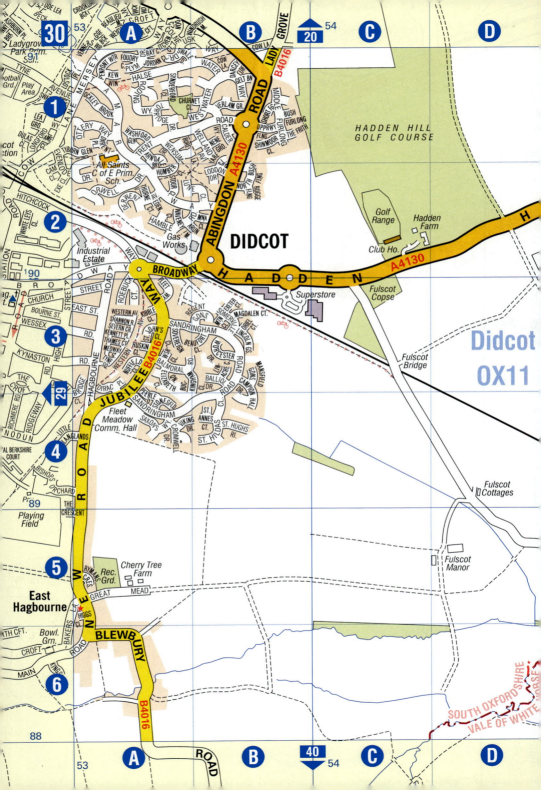

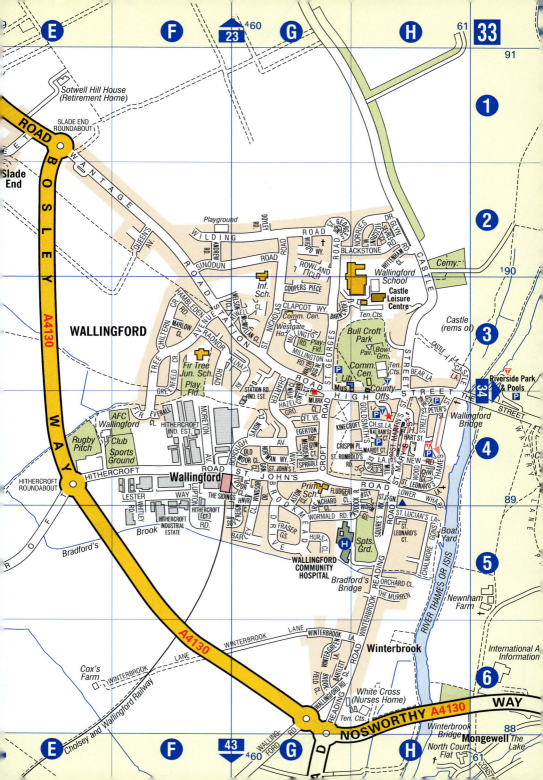

34 61   91

A   **B**   **24** 62   **C**   **D**

1

Preston
Crowmarsh

BENSON AIRFIELD

Lower Farm
Orchard

Crowmarsh
Battle Farm

Riverside

2

Sewage
Works

RIVER THAMES OR ISIS

Howbery Park
Hydraulics Research
Station

Marsh
Wood

Cemy.

190

Castle
(rems of)

Pond

Wallingford

3

CASTLE LA

BEAR LA

Institute of
Hydrology

OX10

Shepherds
Cottage

Riverside Park
& Pools

Playing
Field

33

Wallingford
Bridge

Council
Offs.

Pav.

WINTER'S FLD.

HOWBERY FM.

THE LIMES

**CROWMARSH
GIFFORD**

4

Caravan
Park

NEWNHAM
MURREN
CFT.

THAMES

HOM'S
FM.

Caravan
Park

LANE END

89

Crowmarsh Gifford
C of E Prim. Sch.

CROWMARSH   HILL A413

Boat
Yard

Newnham
Manor
Farm

PARK
VIEW

Hill
Meadow

5

Newnham
Farm

International Agricultural
Information Centre

READING ROAD

A4074

Loneso
Farm

6

brook

WAY

NOSWORTHY   A4130   **WAY**

88
nterbrook
Bridge

North Court
Flat

The
Lake

A
Mongewell

61

PORT

B
Larkrise

62

C

D

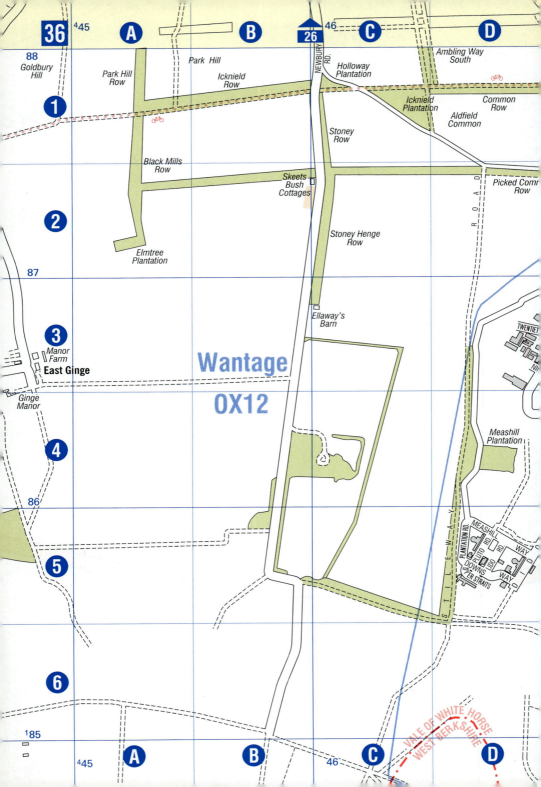

A

B

26

C

D

88
Goldbury
Hill

Park Hill

Park Hill
Row

Icknield
Row

NEWBURY RD.

Holloway
Plantation

Ambling Way
South

Icknield
Plantation

Aldfield
Common

Common
Row

1

Stoney
Row

Black Mills
Row

Skeets
Bush
Cottages

Stoney Henge
Row

Picked Comr
Row

ROAD

2

87

Stoney Henge
Row

Ellaway's
Barn

3

Manor
Farm

East Ginge

TWENTIET
NI

Ginge
Manor

Wantage

OX12

Meashill
Plantation

4

86

STILEWAY

Meashill
PLANTATION RD.
LLWD RD.
UDO
MEASHILL
RD.
WAY

DOWNS
ER STRATS

WAY

5

6

185

445

A

B

46

C

D

VALE OF WHITE HORSE
WEST BERKSHIRE

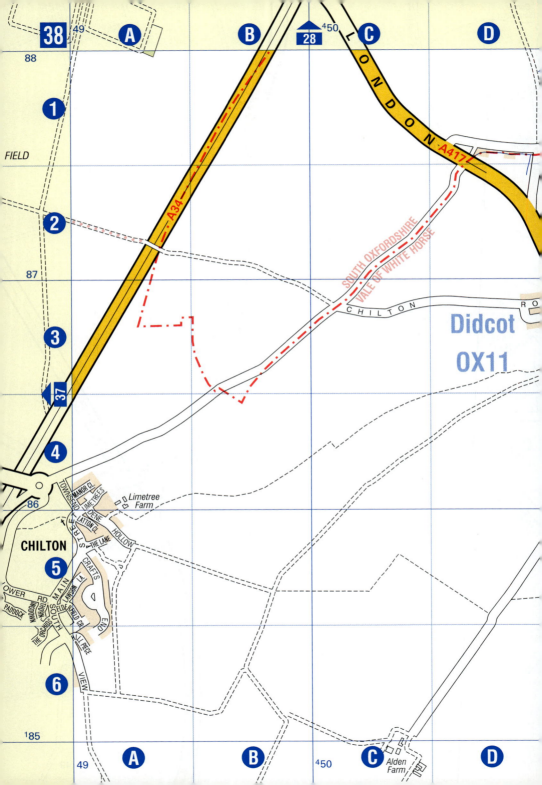

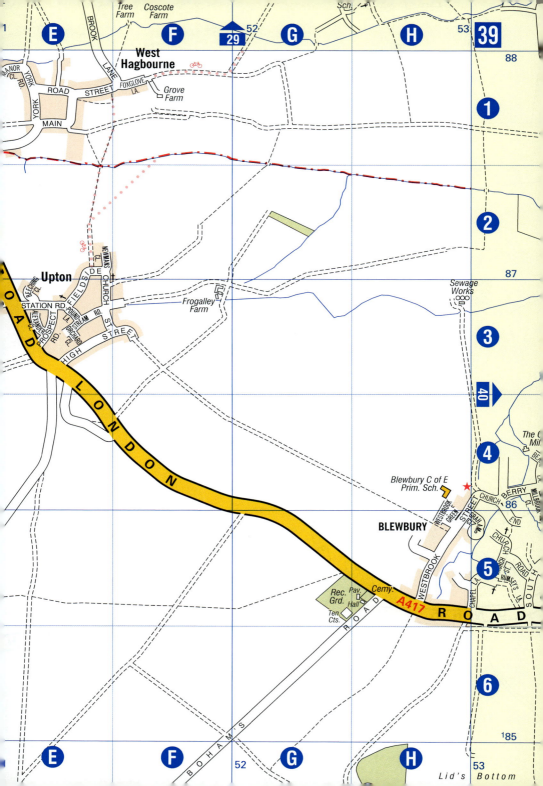

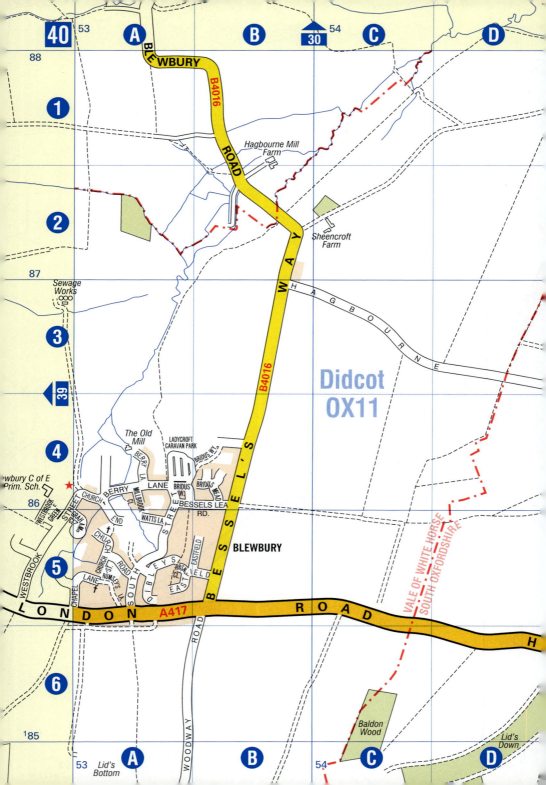

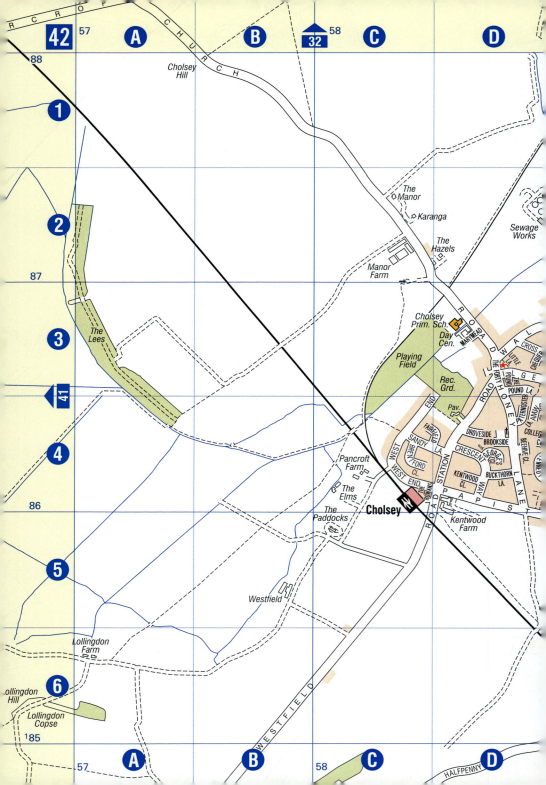

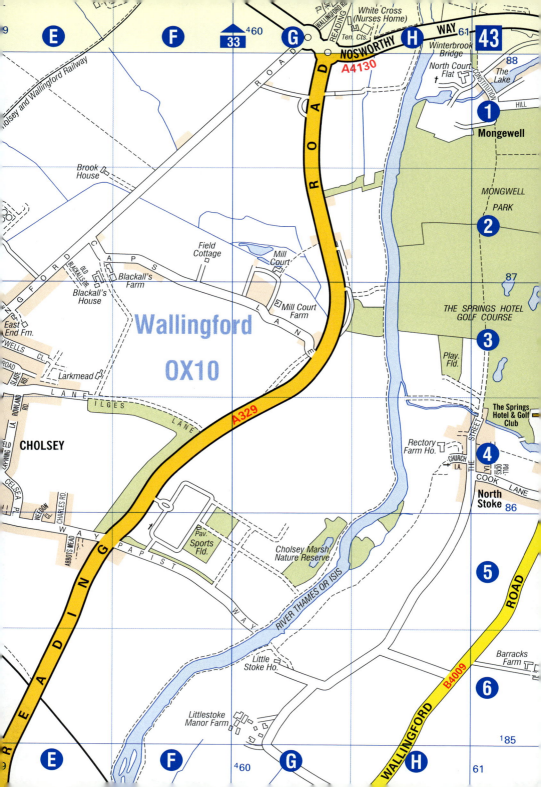

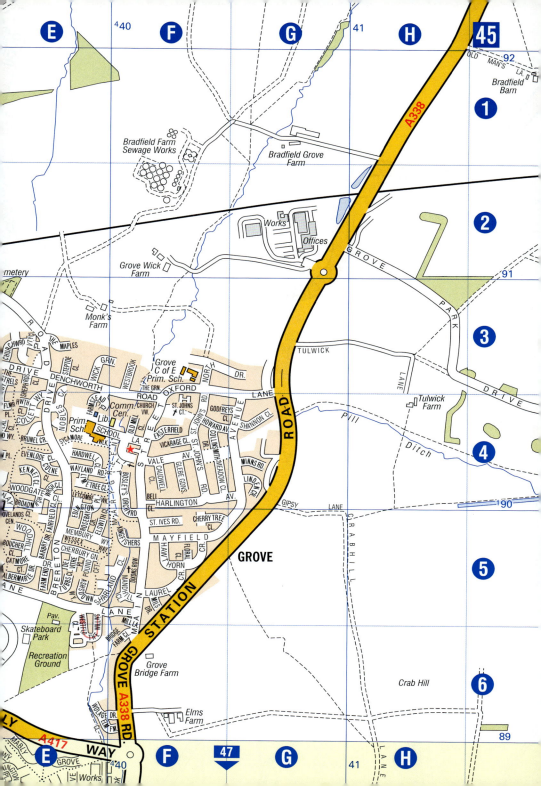

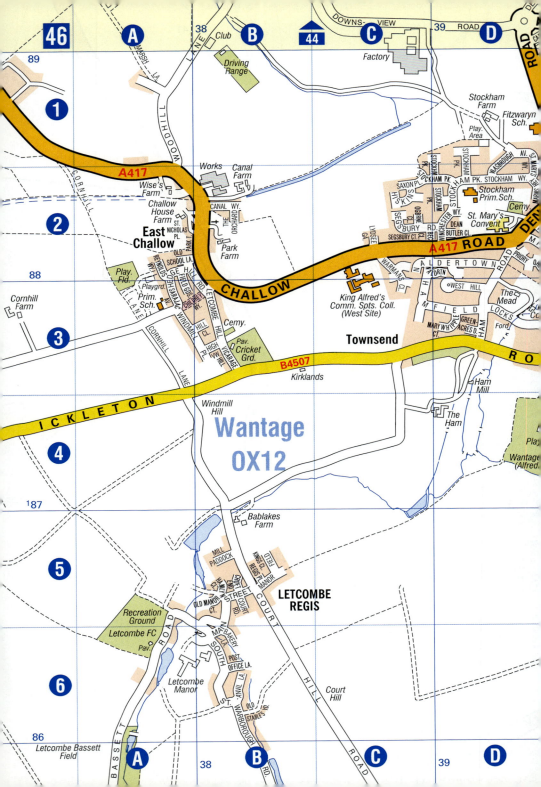

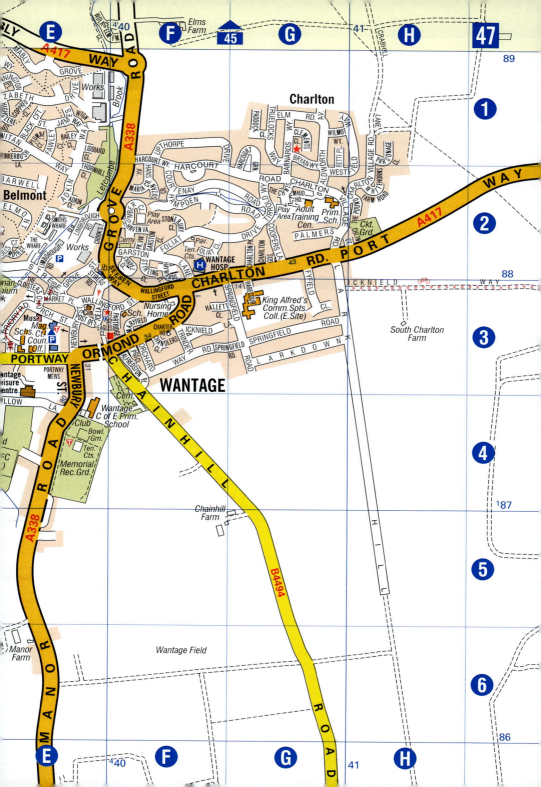

INDEX

Including Streets, Places & Areas, Hospitals & Hospices, Industrial Estates,
Selected Flats & Walkways, Stations and Selected Places of Interest.

HOW TO USE THIS INDEX

1. Each street name is followed by its Postcode District and then by its Locality abbreviation(s) and then by its map reference;
   e.g. **Abbey Cl.** OX14: Abin . . . .6B **6** is in the OX14 Postcode District and the Abingdon Locality and is to be found in square 6B on page **6**. The page number is shown in bold type.

2. A strict alphabetical order is followed in which Av., Rd., St., etc. (though abbreviated) are read in full and as part of the street name;
   e.g. **Baker St.** appears after **Bakers La.** but before **Bakery La.**

3. Streets and a selection of flats and walkways too small to be shown on the maps, appear in the index with the thoroughfare to which it is connected shown in brackets; e.g. **Alfred St.** OX12: Wan . . . .3E **47** (off Mill St.)

4. Addresses that are in more than one part are referred to as not continuous.

5. Places and areas are shown in the index in BLUE TYPE and the map reference is to the actual map square in which the town centre or area is located and not to the place name shown on the map; e.g. **ABINGDON** 6B **6**

6. An example of a selected place of interest is **Benson Veteran Cycle Mus.** 4C **24**

7. An example of a station is **Appleford Station (Rail)** 1H **19**

8. An example of a hospital or hospice is **ABINGDON HOSPITAL** 6G **5**

GENERAL ABBREVIATIONS

Av. : Avenue	**Flds.** : Fields	**La.** : Lane	**Shop.** : Shopping
Bus. : Business	**Gdns.** : Gardens	**Lit.** : Little	**Sq.** : Square
Cvn. : Caravan	**Gth.** : Garth	**Mnr.** : Manor	**St.** : Street
Cen. : Centre	**Ga.** : Gate	**M.** : Mews	**Ter.** : Terrace
Cl. : Close	**Gt.** : Great	**Mus.** : Museum	**Up.** : Upper
Cotts. : Cottages	**Grn.** : Green	**Nth.** : North	**Va.** : Vale
Ct. : Court	**Gro.** : Grove	**No.** : Number	**Vw.** : View
Cres. : Crescent	**Hgts.** : Heights	**Pk.** : Park	**Vs.** : Villas
Cft. : Croft	**Ho.** : House	**Pl.** : Place	**Wlk.** : Walk
Dr. : Drive	**Ind.** : Industrial	**Ri.** : Rise	**W.** : West
Est. : Estate	**Info.** : Information	**Rd.** : Road	**Yd.** : Yard
Fld. : Field	**Intl.** : International	**Rdbt.** : Roundabout	

LOCALITY ABBREVIATIONS

Abin : **Abingdon**	Cos : **Coscote**	Gro : **Grove**	Row : **Rowstock**
App : **Appleford**	Cot : **Cothill**	Har : **Harwell**	Shil : **Shillingford**
A Tir : **Aston Tirrold**	C Gif : **Crowmarsh Gifford**	L Bas : **Letcombe Bassett**	S Hil : **Shillingford Hill**
A Upt : **Aston Upthorpe**	Cul : **Culham**	L Reg : **Letcombe Regis**	Ship : **Shippon**
Bay : **Bayworth**	Den : **Denchworth**	Lit W : **Little Wittenham**	S Mor : **South Moreton**
Ben : **Benson**	Did : **Didcot**	Lon W : **Long Wittenham**	Spri : **Springwell**
Ber : **Berinsfield**	D Tha : **Dorchester-on-Thames**	Marc : **Marcham**	Stev : **Steventon**
Ber S : **Berrick Salome**	Dray : **Drayton**	Milt : **Milton**	S Cou : **Sutton Courtenay**
Bes : **Besslesleigh**	D Leo : **Drayton St Leonard**	M Hil : **Milton Hill**	Upt : **Upton**
Blew : **Blewbury**	D San : **Dry Sandford**	Mon : **Mongewell**	Wal : **Wallingford**
B Bal : **Brightwell Baldwin**	E Cha : **East Challow**	Moul : **Moulsford**	Wan : **Wantage**
B Sot : **Brightwell-cum-Sotwell**	E Hag : **East Hagbourne**	N'ton : **Newington**	War : **Warborough**
Bri S : **Britwell Salome**	E Hen : **East Hendred**	N Mor : **North Moreton**	W Hag : **West Hagbourne**
Bur : **Burcot**	Ewel : **Ewelme**	N Sto : **North Stoke**	W Hen : **West Hendred**
Chil : **Chilton**	F Hea : **Frilford Heath**	N Cou : **Nuneham Courtenay**	W Loc : **West Lockinge**
Chol : **Cholsey**	Goo : **Goosey**	Rad : **Radley**	
C Ham : **Clifton Hampden**	G For : **Gozzard's Ford**	Rok : **Roke**	

A

Abbey Brook OX11: Did 6G **19**
Abbey Cl. OX14: Abin 6B **6**
Abbey Meadows 6C **6**
Abbey Sailing Club 2B **10**
Abbey Sports Cen. 2A **14**
Abbey Woods Cl.
  OX10: Ber 2A **14**
Abbots Mead OX10: Chol 5E **43**
Abbott Rd. OX11: Did 4G **29**
  OX14: Abin 5B **6**
ABINGDON 6B **6**
Abingdon Abbey (remains of)
  . . . . .6B **6**
    (off Bridge St.)
Abingdon Bus. Pk.
  OX14: Abin 5G **5**

ABINGDON HOSPITAL 6G **5**
Abingdon Mus. 6B **6**
    (off Market Pl.)
Abingdon Rd.
  OX10: D Tha 3H **13**
  OX11: Did 2B **30**
  OX13: Stev 4E **17**
  OX14: Bur, C Ham, Cul
  . . . . .1C **10**
  OX14: Dray 6F **9**
  OX14: S Cou 5D **10**
Abingdon Rowing Club 2B **10**
Abingdon Ter. OX11: Did 3E **29**
Abingford By-Pass
  OX14: Dray 5E **9**
  OX14: Dray, Milt 3F **17**
Abott Cl. OX11: Did 4G **29**
Adkin Way OX12: Wan 2E **47**
Albermarle Dr. OX12: Gro . . .5E **45**

Aldridge Cl. OX10: Ben 5C **24**
  OX14: Abin 3B **6**
Aldworth Av. OX12: Wan 2G **47**
Alexander Cl. OX11: Upt 3E **39**
  OX14: Abin 2C **6**
Alfredston Pl.
  OX12: Wan 3F **47**
Alfred St. OX12: Wan 3E **47**
Alister Taylor Av.
  OX10: Ben 1E **35**
Allder Cl. OX14: Abin 3B **6**
Allin's La. OX12: E Hen 4B **26**
Allnatt Av. OX10: Wal 3G **33**
All Saints Cl. OX13: Marc 1A **8**
All Saints Ct. OX11: Did 1G **29**
All Saints La.
  OX14: S Cou 6C **10**
Alphin Brook OX11: Did 6G **19**
Amwell Pl. OX10: Chol 4D **42**

Amyce Cl. OX14: Abin 3D **6**
    (off Yeld Hall Rd.)
Ancholme Cl. OX11: Did 1H **29**
Anchor La. OX11: S Mor 1G **41**
Andersey Way OX14: Abin . . .3A **10**
Andover Rd. OX10: Ben 6F **25**
Andrew Rd. OX10: Wal 2F **33**
Anna Pavlova Cl.
  OX14: Abin 6H **5**
Anson Cl. OX13: Marc 1B **8**
Anson Rd. OX10: Ben 6F **25**
Anthony Hill Rd.
  OX10: Ben 2D **34**
Anvil La. OX12: L Reg 6B **46**
APPLEFORD 1H **19**
Appleford Dr. OX14: Abin 3C **6**
Appleford Rd.
  OX14: S Cou 6D **10**
Appleford Station (Rail) . . .1H **19**

Argentan Cl. OX14: Abin 3H 9
Argosy Rd. OX10: Ben 6F 25
Arndale Beck OX11: Did 1A 30
Arun M. OX11: Did 2B 30
Ashburn Pl. OX11: Did 6H 19
Ashdown Way
   OX12: Gro 5E 45
Ashenden Cl. OX14: Abin 4B 6
Ashgate OX14: Abin 3A 10
   (off Kensington Cl.)
Ashmole Rd. OX14: Abin 3A 10
Aston Cl. OX10: Wal 4G 33
   OX14: Abin 6B 6
Aston St. OX11: A Tir 5F 41
Atwell Cl. OX10: Wal 3G 33
Audlett Dr. OX14: Abin 6C 6
Austin Pl. OX14: Abin 3A 6
Avenue, The OX10: S Hil 5F 23
Avon Rd. OX11: Chil 4G 37
   OX13: Ship 2G 5
Avon Way OX11: Did 6H 19

B

Baden Powell Way
   OX11: Did 3G 29
Badgers Copse
   OX14: Rad 3G 7
Bailey Cl. OX12: Wan 1E 47
Bailie Cl. OX14: Abin 1A 10
Baker Cl. OX10: Ben 1F 35
Baker Rd. OX14: Abin 3A 10
Bakers La. OX10: B Sot 1D 32
   OX11: E Hag 6H 29
Baker St. OX11: A Tir 4E 41
Bakery La. OX12: L Reg 6B 46
Balfour Cotts. OX14: Bur 2G 13
Ballard Chase
   OX14: Abin 2B 6
Balliol Dr. OX11: Did 3B 30
Balmoral Rd. OX11: Did 3A 30
Banbury Ct. OX14: Abin 6B 6
   (off Vineyard)
Bankside OX12: W Hen 5A 26
Barbury Dr. OX12: Gro 5E 45
Barfleur Cl. OX14: Abin 2D 6
Bargus Cl. OX13: Stev 5E 17
Barley Cl. OX10: Wal 5G 33
Barley Flds. OX11: Did 3E 29
Barnards Way
   OX12: Wan 2G 47
Barn Cl. OX12: Den 1A 44
Barncroft OX10: Wal 3G 33
Barnes Cl. OX11: Did 4G 29
Barnes Rd. OX11: Did 5G 29
Barnett Rd. OX13: Stev 4D 16
Barnett Way OX10: Ben 1F 35
Barrett's Way
   OX14: S Cou 3B 18
Barrington Cl. OX10: Ber 1A 14
Barrow Hill Cl.
   OX14: Abin 3E 7
Barrow La. OX11: Har 4A 28
Barrow Rd. OX11: Har 3A 28
   OX13: Ship 5E 5
Bartlett Cl. OX10: Wal 6G 33
Barton La. OX14: Abin 6D 6
Barwell OX12: Wan 2E 47
Basil Hill Rd. OX11: Did 6F 19
Bassett Rd.
   OX12: L Bas 6A 46
Bath St. OX14: Abin 5A 6
   (not continuous)
Battle Rd. OX10: Ben 1F 35
Beagle Cl. OX14: Abin 3E 7
Bear La. OX10: Wal 3H 33
   OX11: N Mor 4G 31
Beaufort Cl. OX11: Did 3B 30
Beaulieu M. OX11: Did 6A 20
Bec Cl. OX12: Wan 2C 46

Beckett Ho. OX12: Wan 3F 47
   (off Wallingford St.)
Becquerel Av. OX11: Har 3E 37
Beechcroft OX10: D Tha 6B 14
Beeching Cl. OX11: Upt 3E 39
Beech Rd. OX10: S Hil 5F 23
Beehive Cl. OX10: Chol 4D 42
Beggarsbush Hill
   OX10: Ben 1E 35
Belfast Rd. OX10: Ben 6F 25
Bell Cl. OX12: Gro 4F 45
Bell La. OX10: B Sot 1C 32
BELMONT 2E 47
Belmont OX12: Wan 2E 47
BENSON 5B 24
Benson La. OX10: C Gif 4B 34
Benson Rd. OX14: Abin 3A 6
Benson Veteran Cycle Mus.
   . . . . .4C 24
Bergen Av. OX14: Abin 3H 9
Berinscourt Ho.
   OX10: Ber 2H 13
BERINSFIELD 2A 14
Berinsfield Rdbt.
   OX10: Ber 3H 13
BERRICK SALOME 1C 24
Berry Cft. OX14: Abin 4A 6
Berry La. OX11: Blew 4A 40
Bessels Lea Rd.
   OX11: Blew 4A 40
Bessel's Way OX11: Blew . . .5B 40
Beverley Cl. OX14: Abin 4A 6
Beverly Cl. OX10: Ben 6F 25
Binning Cl. OX14: Dray 1F 17
Birmingham Yd.
   OX10: Ben 5B 24
Bishops Orchard
   OX11: E Hag 4H 29
Black Cft. OX12: Wan 1E 47
Blackhorse La.
   OX13: Cot, G For 2C 4
Blacklands Rd.
   OX10: Ben 4C 24
Blacklands Way
   OX14: Abin 6G 5
Blacknall Rd. OX14: Abin 2A 10
Blackstone Rd.
   OX10: Wal 2G 33
Blackwater Way
   OX11: Did 6A 20
Blagrave Cl. OX11: Did 2G 29
Blakehope Burn
   OX11: Did 6H 19
Blakes Fld. OX11: Did 2F 29
Blecher Ct. OX10: D Tha 5B 14
Blenheim Cl. OX11: Did 2G 29
Blenheim Gdns.
   OX12: Gro 4D 44
Blenheim Hill OX11: Har 4B 28
Blenheim Pl. OX10: Ben 6F 25
Blenheim Riding Cen. 6F 35
BLEWBURY 5A 40
Blewbury Rd.
   OX11: E Hag 6A 30
Boham's Rd. OX11: Blew 6F 39
Boreford Rd. OX14: Abin 3D 6
Borough Av. OX10: Wal 4G 33
Borough Wlk. OX14: Abin 4A 6
Bosley Cres. OX10: Wal 4H 33
Bosley's Orchard
   OX11: Did 2G 29
   OX12: Gro 4F 45
Bosley Way OX10: Wal 2E 33
Bostock Rd. OX14: Abin 6A 6
Botany Gdns. OX10: C Gif . . .5C 34
Bothy Vineyard 3A 4
Boucher Cl. OX12: Gro 5E 45
Boulter Dr. OX14: Abin 2C 6
Bourlon Wood OX14: Abin . . .4H 5
Bourne St. OX11: Did 3H 29
Bowgrave Copse
   OX14: Abin 4E 7
Bowmont Water
   OX11: Did 1G 29

Bowness Av. OX11: Did 4F 29
Bowyer Rd. OX14: Abin 5B 6
Boxhill Rd. OX14: Abin 5B 6
Boxhill Wlk. OX14: Abin 5A 6
Boxwell Cl. OX14: Abin 3D 6
Bradstock's Way
   OX14: S Cou 3B 18
Brampton Cl. OX14: Abin 4A 6
Brasenose Rd. OX11: Did 2E 29
Braze La. OX10: Ben 4D 24
Brendon Cl. OX11: Did 1E 29
Brent Av. OX11: Did 5H 19
Brentford Cl. OX10: Chol 4C 42
Brereton Dr. OX12: Gro 5E 45
Brewer Cl. OX13: Stev 5E 17
Brewers Cl. OX11: Did 1B 10
Bridge Cl. OX11: Did 3A 30
BRIDGE END 1B 22
Bridge End OX10: D Tha 6B 14
Bridge Farm Cl.
   OX12: Gro 6F 45
Bridge Ho. Cvn. Pk.
   OX14: C Ham 4D 12
Bridges Cl. OX11: Abin 2G 9
Bridge St. OX14: Abin 6B 6
Bridus Mead OX11: Blew 4B 40
Bridus Way OX11: Blew 4A 40
BRIGHTWELL-CUM-SOTWELL
   . . . . .6C 22
Brightwell St.
   OX10: B Sot 1B 32
Britwell Rd. OX10: Ewel 5H 25
   OX11: Did 2G 29
Brixton Hill OX10: Ben 6H 35
Broadmarsh Cl.
   OX12: Gro 4E 45
Broad St. OX14: Abin 6B 6
Broadway OX11: Did 3G 29
   OX11: Har 5A 28
Broadway Cl. OX11: Har 5A 28
Brode Cl. OX14: Abin 4A 6
Brookfield Cl. OX10: Wal 6G 33
Brook La.
   OX11: Cos, W Hag 6E 29
   OX12: Den 1B 44
Brookmead Dr.
   OX10: Wal 4G 33
Brookside OX10: Chol 4D 42
   OX11: Har 4A 28
   OX14: Abin 4B 6
Brook St. OX10: Ben 5C 24
   OX14: S Cou 1B 18
Brunel Cres. OX12: Gro 4E 45
Brunel Rd. OX11: Did 3E 29
Brunstock Beck
   OX11: Did 6H 19
Bryan Way OX12: Wan 1G 47
Buckingham Cl.
   OX11: Did 3A 30
Buckland M. OX14: Abin 6H 5
   (off Winterborne Rd.)
Bucklers Bury Rd.
   OX14: Abin 2D 6
Buckles Cl. OX14: Abin 6H 5
Buckner's Cl. OX10: Ben 5B 24
Buckthorn La.
   OX10: Chol 4D 42
Bulldog Cl. OX10: Ben 1D 34
Bullingdon Av.
   OX10: Ber 2A 14
BURCOT 3G 13
Burcot La. OX10: D Tha 3B 14
Burcot Pk. OX14: Bur 2F 13
Bure La. OX11: Did 1A 30
Burgess Cl. OX14: Abin 6B 6
Burrows Hill OX10: Ewel 6H 25
Burr St. OX11: Har 4A 28
Burton Cl. OX14: Abin 1H 9
Burycroft, The
   OX14: Cul 3C 10
Bury St. OX14: Abin 6B 6
Buscot Dr. OX14: Abin 3D 6
Bush Furlong OX11: Did 1B 30
Byron Cl. OX14: Abin 2G 9

C

CALDECOTT 2A 10
Caldecott Cl. OX14: Abin 1H 9
Caldecott Ct. OX14: Abin 1H 9
   (off Caldecott Cl.)
Caldecott Rd. OX14: Abin 1H 9
Calder Way OX11: Did 1B 30
Caldicott Cl. OX10: Shil 3F 23
Cam Cl. OX11: Did 2H 29
Cameron Av. OX14: Abin 4E 7
Campion Hall Dr.
   OX11: Did 3B 30
Campion Rd. OX14: Abin 5D 6
Canal Cl. OX14: Abin 6D 44
Canal Ho. OX12: Wan 2E 47
   (off Smiths Wharf)
Canal Way OX12: E Cha 2B 46
Cane La. OX12: Gro 5E 45
Caps La. OX10: Chol 2E 43
Carlton Cl. OX12: Gro 4D 44
Carse Cl. OX14: Abin 2D 6
Castle Cl. OX10: Ben 5B 24
Castle La. OX10: Wal 3H 33
Castle Leisure Cen. 3H 33
Castle Sq. OX10: Ben 5B 24
Castle St. OX10: Wal 2H 33
   OX13: Stev 6D 16
Castle Way OX11: Did 1G 29
Catharine Cl. OX14: Rad 2H 7
Cat La. OX10: Ewel 5H 25
Catmore Cl. OX12: Gro 5E 45
Caudwell Cl. OX12: Gro 4F 45
   OX14: Dray 6F 9
Causeway, The
   OX13: Stev 5D 16
   (not continuous)
Cedars, The OX10: Ben 4C 24
Celsea Pl. OX10: Chol 4E 43
Cemetery Rd.
   OX14: Abin 6H 5
Chainhill Rd. OX12: Wan 3F 47
Chalk Hill OX11: A Tir 6F 41
Challenor Cl. OX14: Abin 3A 10
Challow Rd.
   OX12: E Cha, Wan 3B 46
Chalmore Gdns.
   OX10: Wal 5H 33
Chambrai Cl. OX14: App 1H 19
Champs Chapel Mus. 5C 26
Champs Cl. OX14: Abin 3E 7
Chancel Way OX13: Marc 6A 4
Chandlers Cl. OX12: Wan 3F 47
   OX14: Abin 4E 7
Chapel Cl. OX12: Wan 2F 47
Chapel La. OX10: Ben 5B 24
   OX10: Rok 2D 24
   OX11: Blew 5A 40
   OX14: S Cou 1C 18
Chapel Sq. OX12: E Hen 5B 26
Charles Rd. OX10: Chol 5E 43
CHARLTON 1G 47
Charlton Av. OX14: Abin 2H 47
Charlton Gdns.
   OX12: Wan 2G 47
Charlton Pk. OX12: Wan 2G 47
Charlton Rd. OX12: Wan 3F 47
Charlton Village Rd.
   OX12: Wan 2G 47
Charney Av. OX14: Abin 3D 6
Charter Ho. OX12: Wan 3F 47
Charter Way OX10: Wal 3G 33
Chaucer Cl. OX10: Ewel 5H 25
Chaunterell Way
   OX14: Abin 1G 9
Checker Wlk. OX14: Abin 6B 6
Cheers Farm OX14: Dray 6G 9
Chequers Pl. OX10: Chol 3D 42
Cherbury Grn. OX12: Gro 5E 45
Cherry Cl. OX10: Shil 3E 23
Cherry Tree Cl. OX12: Gro . . .5F 45
Cherry Tree Ct. OX11: Har . . .4A 28

Cherry Tree Dr. OX13: Ship 3G 5
Cherwell Cl. OX10: Wal 4H 33
  OX11: Did 5H 19
  OX14: Abin 4D 6
Cherwell Rd. OX10: Ber 1A 14
Chestnut Av. OX14: Rad 1G 7
Chestnuts, The
  OX12: Wan 2G 47
  OX14: Abin 4E 7
Chestnut Tree Cl.
  OX13: Ship 4G 5
Cheyney Wlk. OX14: Abin 4A 6
Chiers Dr. OX14: Dray 6G 9
Childrey Way
  OX12: E Cha 3A 46
  OX14: Abin 3D 6
Chillbrook OX11: Har 5A 28
Chiltern Cl. OX10: Ben 5B 24
  OX10: Ber 2A 14
Chiltern Cres. OX10: Wal . . .3F 33
CHILTON 5H 37
Chilton Cl. OX14: Abin 4D 6
Chilton Rd. OX11: Upt 3C 38
Chinnock Brook
  OX11: Did 6H 19
Chipmunk Rd. OX10: Ben . .6F 25
CHOLSEY 3D 42
Cholsey and Wallingford Railway
  Cholsey Station 4C 42
  Wallingford Station 4F 33
Cholsey Marsh Nature Reserve
  . . . . .5G 43
Cholsey Station
  Cholsey and
  Wallingford Railway . . .4C 42
Cholsey Station (Rail) 4C 42
Cholswell Ct. OX13: Ship . . .2G 5
Cholswell Rd. OX13: Ship . . .4G 5
Church Cl. OX11: E Hag 6H 29
Church End OX11: Blew 4A 40
Churchfield La.
  OX10: Ben 5A 24
           (not continuous)
Churchill Cl. OX11: Did 2E 29
Churchill Rd. OX11: Did 2E 29
Church La. OX13: B Sot 1B 32
  OX10: D Leo 2F 15
  OX10: N Sto 4H 43
  OX10: Wal 4H 33
  OX11: Har 4A 28
  OX11: S Mor 6F 31
  OX13: D San 1D 4
  OX14: Dray 6G 9
Churchmere Rd.
  OX14: S Cou 6C 10
Church Rd. OX10: Ben 5A 24
  OX10: Chol 6A 32
  OX11: Blew 5A 40
  OX14: Rad 2G 7
Church St. OX11: Blew 5A 40
  OX11: Did 3H 29
  OX11: Upt 3E 39
  OX12: E Hen 5B 26
  OX12: Wan 3E 47
  OX13: Marc 1A 8
  OX14: App 1H 19
  OX14: S Cou 6C 10
Church Vw. OX10: Ber 2A 14
  OX12: Gro 4F 45
Church Vw. Ho.
  OX12: Wan 2E 47
        (off Smiths Wharf)
Church Wlk. OX14: Rad 2G 7
Churchward Cl. OX11: Did . . .5F 19
Churchward Cl.
  OX12: Gro 3E 45
Churnet Cl. OX11: Did 1A 30
Circourt Rd.
  OX12: Den, E Cha 4A 44
Clack's La. OX10: C Gif 4C 34
Clapcot Way OX10: Wal 3G 33
Clarence Pl. OX11: Did 4G 29
Clarendon Cl. OX14: Abin . . .5D 6

Clay La. OX10: Ben 1E 35
Cleave, The OX11: Har 4A 28
Clements Cl. OX12: Wan 1G 47
Clements Grn.
  OX11: S Mor 6F 31
Clevelands OX14: Abin 4C 6
Clifton Dr. OX14: Abin 5B 6
CLIFTON HAMPDEN 3D 12
Cloisters, The OX10: Ewel . .6H 25
  OX12: Wan 3E 47
Close, The OX10: Ben 4B 24
  OX11: A Tir 5F 41
Coach Way OX10: Ben 5B 24
Cobden Cen., The
  OX11: Did 5G 19
Cochrane Rd. OX10: Ben . . .2F 35
Cockcroft Rd. OX11: Did 5G 29
Colborne Rd. OX11: Did 3F 29
Cole Ct. OX11: Did 6H 19
Coleridge Dr. OX14: Abin . . .2H 9
College Cl. OX10: Chol 4D 42
College Farm OX10: Ben . . .5B 24
Collett OX11: Did 6G 19
Collett Way OX12: Gro 4E 45
Collingwood Cl.
  OX14: Abin 4B 6
Collingwood Rd.
  OX11: Did 3E 29
Collinsmith Dr. OX12: Gro . .4F 45
Colne Cl. OX12: Gro 4E 45
Colne Dr. OX10: Ber 1B 14
  OX11: Did 6A 20
Coln Rd. OX11: Har 2F 37
Columbia Way OX12: Gro . . .5D 44
Colwell Cl. OX14: Abin 5G 5
Colwell Dr. OX10: Ber 1A 14
Colwell Rd. OX10: Ber 1A 14
Compton Dr OX14: Abin 2D 6
Compton Ter. OX10: Wal . . .4G 33
Conduit Rd. OX14: Abin 6A 6
Constitution Hill
  OX10: Mon 1H 43
Conway Rd. OX13: Ship 3H 5
Cook La. OX10: N Sto 4H 43
Coopers La. OX12: Wan 2G 47
  OX14: Abin 1A 10
Coopers Piece OX10: Wal . . .3G 33
Copenhagen Dr.
  OX14: Abin 5G 5
Copperfield Cl.
  OX12: Wan 1E 47
Copse, The OX14: Abin 4E 7
Corn Avill Cl. OX14: Abin . . .3E 7
Corneville Rd. OX14: Dray . . .5F 9
Corn Exchange, The (Theatre)
  . . . . .4H 33
          (off Market Pl.)
Cornhill La. OX12: E Cha . . .2A 46
Coromandel OX14: Abin 3H 9
COSCOTE 6F 29
COTHILL 1C 4
Cothill National Nature Reserve
  . . . . .1B 4
Cothill Rd. OX13: Cot 3B 4
Cotman Cl. OX14: Abin 2A 10
Cotswold Pk. OX11: Did 1E 29
Cottesmore La.
  OX10: Ewel 4F 25
Coulings Cl.
  OX12: E Hen 4B 26
Court, The OX14: Abin 4A 6
Court Dr. OX10: Shil 4F 23
Courtenay Cl.
  OX14: S Cou 2C 18
Courtenay Rd. OX12: Wan . .2F 47
Court Hill Rd.
  OX12: L Reg, Wan 5B 46
Courtiers Grn.
  OX14: C Ham 3D 12
Covent Cl. OX12: L Reg 5B 46
Covent Cl. OX14: Abin 2D 6
Cow La. OX11: Did 1B 30
             (Halse Water)
  OX11: Did 2H 29
             (Station Rd.)

Cow La. OX11: Did, Har 3B 28
  OX13: G For 5C 4
  OX14: Milt 2B 28
  SN7: Den, Goo 1A 44
Cox's La.
  OX10: Ben, C Gif 5C 34
Crabhill La.
  OX12: Gro, Wan 5H 45
Crabtree La. OX14: Dray 5F 9
Crabtree Pl. OX14: Abin 6D 6
Crafts End OX11: Chil 5A 38
Craven Way OX11: Did 4G 29
Cray Ct. OX11: Did 5H 19
Crescent, The
  OX11: E Hag 4H 29
  OX14: Lon W 1D 20
Crescent Way OX10: Chol . . .4D 42
Crispin Pl. OX10: Wal 4G 33
Croasdell Cl. OX14: Abin . . .3A 10
Croft, The OX11: A Tir 4F 41
  OX11: Did 3H 29
  OX11: E Hag 6H 29
  OX11: Har 3A 28
Croft End OX12: L Reg 5B 46
Croft Rd. OX10: Wal 4G 33
Croft Vs. OX10: Wal 4G 33
Cromwell Dr. OX11: Did 4A 30
Cronshaw Cl. OX11: Did 2G 29
Crookdale Beck
  OX11: Did 6A 20
Crook's Ter. OX12: Wan 2E 47
Cross Av. OX10: Ben 1F 35
Cross Cl. OX10: Ben 1G 35
Crosslands Dr. OX14: Abin . . .4A 6
Cross Rd. OX10: Chol 3D 42
Crossville Cres.
  OX11: Did 1F 29
CROWMARSH GIFFORD 4B 34
Crowmarsh Hill
  OX10: C Gif 5C 34
Crown La. OX10: Ben 5B 24
  OX10: D Tha 6B 14
  OX11: S Mor 6G 31
Crown M. OX14: Abin 6A 6
Crutch Furlong
  OX10: Ber 1B 14
CULHAM 4C 10
Culham Cl. OX14: Abin 4C 6
Culham No. 1 Site
  OX14: Cul 4A 12
Culham Science Cen.
  OX14: Cul 3A 12
Culham Station (Rail) 4H 11
Cullen Pl. OX11: Did 3G 29
Cullen Way OX11: Did 3G 29
Cullerne Cl. OX14: Abin 2C 6
Curie Av. OX11: Har 2F 37
Curtis Av. OX14: Abin 6D 6
Curtyn Cl. OX14: Abin 5H 5
Cygnet Cl. OX14: Abin 1A 10
Cyril Wickham Way
  OX12: Gro 5E 45
          (off Cane La.)

D

Dagdale Dr. OX11: Did 6H 19
Daisy Bank OX14: Abin 5D 6
Dalton Av. OX11: Har 3E 37
Dalton Barracks
  OX13: Abin 3F 5
Darcey Lode OX11: Did 1B 30
Darent Pl. OX11: Did 1A 30
Darrell Way OX14: Abin 5B 6
Dart Dr. OX11: Did 6G 19
Dart Rd. OX13: Ship 2G 5
Datchet Grn. OX10: B Sot . .1D 32
Day's La. OX10: Ewel 1G 35
Dean Butler Cl.
  OX12: Wan 2D 46
Deanes Cl. OX13: Stev 6D 16
Dearlove Cl. OX14: Abin 3A 6
DENCHWORTH 1B 44

Denchworth Rd.
  OX12: Den, Gro 2C 44
  OX12: Gro, Wan 2D 46
Dene Hollow OX11: Chil . . .5A 38
Denton Cl. OX14: Abin 5D 6
Derwent Av. OX11: Did 2A 30
Derwent Cl. OX13: Ship 3G 5
De Vitre Pl. OX12: Gro 5E 45
Devon Cl. OX11: Did 6F 25
Dibleys OX11: Blew 5A 40
DIDCOT 2H 29
DIDCOT COMMUNITY HOSPITAL
  . . . . .3E 29
Didcot Leisure Cen. 4H 29
Didcot Parkway Station (Rail)
  . . . . .1H 29
Didcot Railway Cen. 1G 29
Didcot Rd. OX10: B Sot 6A 22
  OX11: Har 4B 28
  OX14: Lon W 1D 20
Didcot Wave, The 4F 29
Dido Rd. OX11: Chil 5D 36
Dirac Pl. OX11: Did 3A 30
Dixons Row OX12: Gro 5F 45
Dodson Ct. OX14: Abin 5B 6
Doe Lea OX11: Did 6H 19
Don Cl. OX11: Did 6A 20
Donnington Pl. OX12: Wan . .1E 47
Dorchester Abbey Mus. . . .6B 14
Dorchester Dr. OX14: Abin . . .4C 6
DORCHESTER ON THAMES
  . . . . .6B 14
Dorchester Rd.
  OX10: D Leo 3C 14
Dorchester Sailing Club . . .4A 14
Downs Cl. OX11: Har 5A 28
Downside OX11: Chil 4G 37
Downs Rd. OX11: Did 4F 29
Downsview Rd.
  OX12: Wan 5C 44
Downs Way OX11: Chil 5D 36
Doyley Rd. OX10: Wal 2G 33
Drake Av. OX11: Did 3F 29
Draysmans Wlk.
  OX14: Abin 1A 10
         (off Coopers La.)
DRAYTON 6F 9
Drayton East Way
  OX14: Dray 1F 17
Drayton Mill OX14: Dray . . .2H 17
Drayton Rd. OX10: D Tha . . .5B 14
         (not continuous)
  OX14: Dray 4G 9
  OX14: Milt 3H 17
  OX14: S Cou 6G 9
DRAYTON ST LEONARD . . .2F 15
Driftway, The OX11: Har . . .4B 28
Drove Side OX10: Chol 4D 42
Druids Wlk. OX11: Did 1G 29
DRY SANDFORD 1D 4
Dry Sandford Nature Reserve
  . . . . .1D 4
Drysdale Cl. OX14: Rad 3G 7
Dudwell Cl. OX11: Did 6G 19
Duffield Cl. OX14: Abin 3D 6
Duffield Pl. OX13: Marc 6A 4
Duke of York Av.
  OX14: Milt 1G 27
Dulas Cl. OX11: Did 1H 29
Dundas Cl. OX14: Abin 5D 6
Dunmore Rd. OX14: Abin . . .3A 6
Dunsden Cl. OX11: Did 2F 29
Dunsomer Hill
  OX11: N Mor 5G 31
Dyer Straits OX11: Chil 5D 36

E

Eagles Cl. OX12: Wan 3E 47
Eason Dr. OX14: Abin 4E 7
Eastbury Cl. *OX12: Wan* . . .2E 47
         (off Smiths Wharf)
EAST CHALLOW 2A 46

Easterfield OX12: Gro 4F **45**
Eastfield OX11: Blew 5A **40**
EAST GINGE **3A 36**
EAST HAGBOURNE **6H 29**
EAST HENDRED **5B 26**
East St Helen St.
   OX14: Abin 1B **10**
East St. OX11: Did 3A **30**
East Way OX14: Dray 1F **17**
Eden Ct. OX11: Did 2A **30**
Eden Cft. OX14: Abin 3C **6**
Edinburgh Dr. OX11: Did . . .2G **29**
Edington Pl. OX12: Gro 5E **45**
Edmonds Ct. OX11: Did 3F **29**
Edward St. OX14: Abin 6H **5**
Edwin Rd. OX11: Did 4F **29**
Egerton Rd. OX10: Wal 4G **33**
Eighteenth St. OX11: Har . . .2E **37**
Eighth St. OX11: Har 2F **37**
Elbourne OX11: Did 3E **29**
Elderfield Cres.
   OX11: Chil 5H **37**
Eleventh St. OX11: Har 3F **37**
Elizabeth Av. OX14: Abin 3E **7**
Elizabeth Dr. OX12: Wan 1E **47**
Elm Bri. Rdbt. OX10: Ben . . .5H **23**
Elm Farm Cl. OX12: Gro 6E **45**
Elm Rd. OX11: N Mor 3G **31**
   OX12: Wan 1G **47**
Elm Tree Wlk. OX13: Ship . . .4G **5**
Elswith Cl. OX12: Gro 5E **45**
Elwes Cl. OX14: Abin 5D **6**
Elwes Rd. OX13: Marc 1B **8**
Ely Cl. OX14: Abin 1G **9**
Eney Cl. OX14: Abin 3E **7**
Ernest Rd. OX11: Did 3G **29**
Euston Way OX12: Wan 5B **44**
Evelin Rd. OX14: Abin 4A **6**
Evenlode Cl. OX12: Gro 4E **45**
Evenlode Dr. OX10: Ber 1A **14**
   OX11: Did 1H **29**
Evenlode Pk. OX14: Abin 4D **6**
EWELME **6H 25**
Exborne Rd. OX14: Abin 6H **5**
Exe Cl. OX11: Did 2H **29**
Exeter Ct. OX11: Did 3B **30**
Eyres Cl. OX10: Ewel 5F **25**
Eyre's La. OX10: Ewel 4F **25**
Eyston Way OX14: Abin 6G **5**

F

Fairacres OX14: Abin 6G **5**
Fairacres Rd. OX11: Did 3G **29**
Fairfield OX10: Chol 4C **42**
Fairfield Cl. OX12: Gro 5E **45**
Fairfield Pl. OX14: Abin 5B **6**
Fane Dr. OX10: Ber 2H **13**
Faraday Av. OX11: Har 3E **37**
   (not continuous)
Faraday Rd. OX12: Wan 5B **44**
Faringdon Rd. OX13: G For . . .3E **5**
   OX13: Ship 4F **5**
   OX14: Abin 4G **5**
Farm End OX12: Gro 5E **45**
Farm Rd. OX14: Abin 3B **6**
Farriers M. OX14: Abin 5C **6**
Farthings, The OX13: Marc . . .6A **4**
Fawley Cl. OX12: Wan 1E **47**
Featherbed La.
   OX11: Row 3D **26**
   OX13: Stev 3D **26**
Fennel Way OX14: Abin 5E **7**
Ferguson Pl. OX14: Abin 5E **7**
Fermi Av. OX11: Chil, Har . . .4E **37**
Ferny Cl. OX14: Rad 2G **7**
Ferry Wlk. OX14: Abin 1B **10**
Fetti Pl. OX12: Wan 1G **47**
Fettiplace Rd.
   OX13: Marc 6B **4**
Fielden Cl. OX10: Ben 1F **35**
Fielden Rd. OX10: Ben 1F **35**

Field Gdns. OX12: E Cha 2A **46**
   OX13: Stev 4E **17**
Fieldside OX11: Upt 3E **39**
   OX14: Abin 4H **5**
   OX14: Lon W 1C **20**
Fifteenth St. OX11: Har 3E **37**
Finham Brook OX11: Did 6H **19**
Finmore Cl. OX14: Abin 5A **6**
Firebrass Hill OX10: Ewel . . .5H **25**
First Av. OX11: Did 1F **29**
First St. OX11: Har 3G **37**
Fir Tree Av. OX10: Wal 4F **33**
Fisher Cl. OX14: Dray 6E **9**
Fishermans Wharf
   OX14: Abin 3B **10**
Fitchett Yd. OX14: Abin 6A **6**
Fitzcount Way OX10: Wal . . .2H **33**
Fitzharris Ind. Est.
   OX14: Abin 4A 6
   (off Thornhill Wlk.)
Fitzharry's Rd. OX14: Abin . .5B **6**
Fleet Way OX11: Did 3A **30**
Floral Cl. OX12: Gro 5F **45**
Fludger Cl. OX10: Wal 4G **33**
Foliat Cl. OX12: Wan 2F **47**
Foliat Dr. OX12: Wan 2F **47**
Ford La. OX10: D Leo 1F **15**
Fordy La. OX12: E Hen 5B **26**
Forge Cl. OX10: Ben 5B **24**
Forty, The OX10: Chol 3D **42**
Foster Rd. OX14: Abin 2B **6**
Foundry Cl. OX11: Did 1A **30**
Fountain Ct. OX14: Abin 5C **6**
Fourteenth St. OX11: Har . . .2F **37**
Fourth St. OX11: Har 2F **37**
Foxborough Rd. OX14: Rad . . .3G **7**
Foxcombe Ct. OX14: Abin . . .5G **5**
Foxglove La. OX11: W Hag . .1F **39**
Foxhall Rd. OX11: Did 2F **29**
Framlands Cl. *OX12: Wan . . .2C 46*
   (off Naldertown)
Francis Lit. Dr. OX14: Abin . .1H **9**
Franklyn Cl. OX14: Abin 3B **6**
Franks La. OX13: Stev 5D **16**
Fraser Gdns. OX10: Wal 5G **33**
Freeman Rd. OX11: Did 2E **29**
Frilford Rd. OX13: Marc 1A **8**
Frilsham St. OX14: S Cou . . .2C **18**
Frith, The OX11: Did 1B **30**
Frome Rd. OX11: Chil 3F **37**
Fullers Rd.
   OX11: A Tir, A Upt 4E **41**
Fullwell Cl. OX14: Abin 4A **6**
Fulmar Pl. OX12: Gro 4E **45**
Fyfield Cl. OX12: Wan 2G **47**

G

Gainsborough Grn.
   OX14: Abin 2H **9**
Gall Cl. OX14: Abin 5E **7**
Galley Fld. OX14: Abin 4D **6**
Gap, The OX13: Marc 1B **8**
Garden Cl. OX11: Did 4F **29**
Gardiner Cl. OX14: Abin 5E **7**
Garford Cl. OX14: Abin 3D **6**
Garston Cl. OX12: Wan 2F **47**
Garston La. OX12: Wan 2F **47**
Garth Rd. OX11: Did 2G **29**
Gaveston Rd. OX11: Har 4A **28**
Gelt Burn OX11: Did 1B **30**
Geoffrey Barbour Rd.
   OX14: Abin 5B **6**
Geoffrey Tuttle Dr.
   OX10: Ben 1D **34**
George Morland Ho.
   OX14: Abin 1B 10
   (off Coopers La.)
Gibson Cl. OX14: Abin 2C **6**
Ginge Cl. OX14: Abin 3D **6**
Gipsy La. OX12: Gro 4G **45**
Glebe, The OX14: Cul 4D **10**
Glebe Gdns. OX12: Gro 4F **45**

Glebe Rd. OX11: Did 3G **29**
Glyme Cl. OX14: Abin 4D **6**
Glyme Dr. OX10: Ber 1B **14**
Glyn Av. OX11: Did 2F **29**
Glyn Rd. OX10: Wal 2H **33**
Godfrey Cl. OX11: Did 1A **10**
Godfreys Cl. OX12: Gro 4F **45**
Godwyn Cl. OX14: Abin 5A **6**
Golafre Rd. OX14: Abin 2A **10**
Goldfinch La. OX10: Chol . . .3D **42**
Goldsmith's La.
   OX10: Wal 4H **33**
Gooch OX11: Did 5G **19**
Gooseacre OX14: Rad 3G **7**
Goose Willow Est.
   OX13: Stev 3A **16**
Gordon Dr. OX14: Abin 4E **7**
GOZZARD'S FORD **3C 4**
Graham Cl. OX11: Blew 5A **40**
Grange Beck OX11: Did 6A **20**
Gravel Cl. OX10: Ben 5B **24**
Gravel La. OX10: War 2F **23**
   OX14: Dray 6F **9**
Gravel Wlk. OX10: D Leo . . .2F **15**
GREAT HOLCOMBE **1H 15**
Great Mead OX11: E Hag . . .5A **30**
Gt. Western Dr. OX11: Did . . .1F **29**
Grebe Cl. OX11: Did 3B **10**
Green, The OX12: Gro 3F **45**
   OX14: Cul 4C **10**
   OX14: Dray 6F **9**
Greenacres OX14: Dray 5F **9**
Greenacres Dr.
   OX12: Wan 3D **46**
Green Cl. OX10: Ben 4C **24**
   OX10: Wal 4G **33**
   OX11: Did 5G **29**
   OX13: Stev 4D **16**
Greenfield Cres.
   OX10: Wal 4F **33**
Green Furlong OX10: Ber 2A **14**
Green La. OX10: Ewel 5F **25**
   OX10: War 2F **23**
   OX13: D San 1E **5**
Greenmere OX10: B Sot 6C **22**
Green Nth., The
   OX10: War 1F **23**
Green Rd. OX10: S Hil 5F **23**
   OX11: Did 4G **29**
Green Sth., The
   OX10: War 1F **23**
Greenway, The
   OX12: W Hen 4A **26**
GROVE **4F 45**
Grove, The OX14: Abin 3D **6**
Grovelands Cen.
   OX12: Gro 5E **45**
Grovelands Ct. *OX12: Gro . . .5E 45*
   (off Princess Gdns.)
Grove La. OX49: Bri S 3H **25**
Grove Pk. Dr.
   OX12: Gro, W Loc 2H **45**
Grove Rd. OX11: Har 3F **27**
   OX12: Gro, Wan 2F **47**
Grove St. OX12: Wan 2E **47**
Grove Technology Pk.
   OX12: Wan 5B **44**
Grundy Cl. OX14: Abin 5D **6**
Guild Ho., The
   OX12: Wan 3F 47
   (off Ormond Rd.)
Gwilym Ct. OX10: Wal 4G **33**

H

Hadden Hill OX11: N Mor . . .2B **30**
Hadland Rd. OX14: Abin 5D **6**
Hagbourne Rd.
   OX11: A Upt, Blew 3C **40**
   OX11: Did 3A **30**
Haines Ct. OX13: Marc 1B **8**
Hale Rd. OX10: Ben 3B **24**
Halfpenny La. OX10: Chol . . .6D **42**

Hallett Cl. OX12: Wan 3F **47**
Halls Cl. OX14: Dray 6G **9**
Halse Water OX11: Did 1A **30**
Hambleden Rd.
   OX10: Wal 3F **33**
Hamble Dr. OX14: Abin 4D **6**
Hamble Rd. OX11: Did 2A **30**
Hamfield OX12: Wan 3C **46**
Hamlyn Cl. OX12: L Reg 5B **46**
Hammer La. OX10: War 5E **15**
Hampden Rd. OX12: Wan . . .2F **47**
Hampden Way
   OX10: Ewel 5H **25**
Ham Rd. OX12: Wan 3D **46**
Hanney Rd. OX13: Stev 3A **16**
Hanover Ct. OX10: Wal 4G **33**
   OX11: Did 4G **29**
Hans Av. OX12: Wan 2F **47**
Hanson Rd. OX14: Abin 2B **6**
Harcourt Grn. OX12: Wan . . .1G **47**
Harcourt Rd. OX12: Wan 2F **47**
Harcourt Way OX12: Wan . . .1F **47**
   OX14: Abin 4B **6**
Harding Rd. OX14: Abin 5H **5**
Hardings Strings
   OX11: Did 4G **29**
Hardwell Cl. OX12: Gro 4E **45**
Harecourt OX12: Wan 3G **47**
Harlington Av. OX12: Gro 4F **45**
Harrier Pk. OX11: Did 5F **19**
Hart Cl. OX14: Abin 5E **7**
Hartley Cl. OX10: Shil 3F **23**
Hart St. OX10: Wal 4H **33**
HARWELL **4A 28**
Harwell Cl. OX14: Abin 4C **6**
Harwell Intl. Bus. Cen.
   OX11: Har 3G **37**
Harwell Rd. OX14: S Cou . . .3B **18**
Harwood Rd.
   OX11: E Hag 5H **29**
Haven Cl. OX10: D Tha 1B **22**
Haven Va. OX12: Wan 2F **47**
Havers Av. OX14: Milt 1H **27**
Hawksworth OX11: Did 5F **19**
Hawksworth Cl.
   OX12: Gro 4E **45**
Hawthorn Cl. OX10: Wal 4G **33**
Hawthorn Cres.
   OX12: Gro 5F **45**
Hawthorne Av. OX13: Abin 3F **5**
Haydon Rd. OX11: Did 2G **29**
Haywards Cl. OX12: Wan 2F **47**
Haywards Rd. OX14: Dray . . .1F **17**
Hazel Gro. OX10: Wal 4G **33**
Healey Cl. OX14: Abin 1A **10**
Hean Cl. OX14: Abin 3D **6**
Heathcote Pl. OX14: Abin 4E **7**
Heather Rd. OX14: Milt 3H **17**
Hedge Hill Rd.
   OX12: E Cha 2A **46**
Hedgemead Av.
   OX14: Abin 4E **7**
Helen's Way OX10: Ben 6B **24**
Hendred Way OX14: Abin 4D **6**
Henfield Vw. OX10: War 1F **23**
Hengest Ga. OX11: Har 4A **28**
Henley Rd.
   OX10: D Tha, Shil 6B **14**
Henleys La. OX14: Dray 6F **9**
Henley Way OX10: Ewel 1H **35**
Henor Mill Cl. OX14: Abin . . .3D **6**
Herman Cl. OX14: Abin 5D **6**
Hermitage Rd. OX14: Abin . . .1H **9**
Heron Ct. OX14: Abin 3B **10**
Heron Rd. OX10: Ben 6F **25**
Heron's Wlk. OX14: Abin 4B **6**
Herringcote OX10: D Tha 5B **14**
Higgs Cl. OX11: E Hag 5A **30**
Highclere Gdns.
   OX12: Wan 1E **47**
High Rd. OX10: B Sot 6C **22**
High St. OX10: Ben 5B **24**
   OX10: D Leo 2F **15**
   OX10: D Tha 5B **14**

High St. OX10: Ewel 5F 25
  OX10: Wal 4G 33
  OX11: Did 3H 29
  OX11: Har 4A 28
  OX11: N Mor 4G 31
  OX11: S Mor 6F 31
  OX11: Upt 3E 39
  OX12: E Hen 5B 26
  OX13: Stev 5E 17
  OX14: Abin 6B 6
  OX14: C Ham 4C 12
  OX14: Cul 4C 10
  OX14: Dray 6F 9
  OX14: Lon W 1C 20
  OX14: Milt 5G 17
  OX14: S Cou 2C 18
High Vw. OX12: E Cha 3B 46
Hillary Dr. OX11: Did 4G 29
Hill Cl. OX12: E Cha 3B 46
Hillers Cl. OX14: S Cou 1C 18
Hilliat Flds. OX14: Dray 6F 9
Hill Piece OX11: Chil 6A 38
Hillside OX11: Har 2E 37
Hillview Rd. OX14: Abin 3B 6
Hillyard Barns
  OX14: S Cou 1B 18
Hiskins OX12: Wan 2C 46
Hitchcock Way
  OX11: Did 2H 29
Hitching Ct. OX14: Abin 6G 5
Hithercroft OX10: Chol 6G 31
  OX11: S Mor 6G 31
Hithercroft Ct. OX10: Wal 5F 33
Hithercroft Ind. Est.
  OX10: Wal 4F 33
  (not continuous)
Hithercroft Rd. OX10: Wal 4E 33
Hithercroft Rdbt.
  OX10: Wal 4E 33
Hobbs Cl. OX14: Abin 5D 6
Hobbyhorse La.
  OX14: S Cou 2C 18
Hogarth Pl. OX14: Abin 2A 10
Holcombe La.
  OX10: N'ton 1H 15
Holland Rd. OX14: Abin 3C 6
Holloway, The OX11: Har 5A 28
Holt, The OX14: Abin 5B 6
Holywell Cl. OX14: Abin 3E 7
Home Farm OX10: C Gif 4B 34
Home Farm Cl.
  OX12: E Hen 4B 26
Honeybottom La.
  OX13: D San 1D 4
Honey La. OX10: Chol 4D 42
Horn La. OX12: E Hen 6B 26
Horseshoes La.
  OX10: Ben 5B 24
Hound Cl. OX14: Abin 3E 7
Howard Av. OX12: Gro 4F 45
Howard Cornish Rd.
  OX13: Marc 6A 4
Howbery Farm
  OX10: C Gif 4B 34
Hudleston Av. OX10: Ben 1E 35
Humber Cl. OX11: Did 2A 30
  OX12: Wan 2F 47
Hungerford Rd.
  OX11: Har, Row 5F 27
  OX12: E Hen 5F 27
  OX13: M Hil 5F 27
Hunter Cl. OX14: Abin 2D 6
Hunters Cl. OX12: Gro 4D 44
Hurst Cl. OX10: Wal 5G 33
Hyde, The OX14: Abin 2H 9
Hyde Copse OX13: Marc 6B 4
Hyde Rd. OX12: Den 1B 44

I

Ickleton Rd.
  OX12: E Cha, Wan 4A 46
Icknield Cl. OX11: Did 2E 29

Icknield La. OX12: Wan 3F 47
Icknield Way OX10: Ben 6F 35
  OX10: Ewel 1H 35
  OX12: Wan 3H 47
Ilges La. OX10: Chol 3D 42
Ingrebourne Way
  OX11: Did 6H 19
Inkerman Cl. OX14: Abin 4H 5
Isis Cl. OX14: Abin 4D 6
Itchen Ct. OX11: Did 6A 20

J

Jackman Cl. OX14: Abin 6C 6
Javelin Way OX10: Ben 6F 25
Jemmetts Cl.
  OX10: D Tha 6B 14
Jennings La. OX11: Har 4A 28
Jenyns Cl. OX14: Abin 1H 9
Jethro Tull Gdns.
  OX10: C Gif 4A 34
John Morris Rd.
  OX14: Abin 2A 10
Jordan Cl. OX11: Did 1A 30
Jubilee Way OX11: Did 4A 30
Juniper Ct. OX14: Abin 1H 9
  (off Ock St.)

K

Katchside OX14: S Cou 3B 18
Kempster Cl. OX14: Abin 5D 6
Kennedy Cres. OX10: Chol 4D 42
Kennel La. OX13: Stev 4E 17
Kennet Cl. OX10: Ber 3A 14
  OX12: Gro 4E 45
Kennet Rd. OX11: Chil 4G 37
  OX14: Abin 4D 6
Kennett Pl. OX11: Did 3A 30
Kennington Rd. OX14: Rad 2G 7
Kensington Cl.
  OX14: Abin 3A 10
Kent Cl. OX14: Abin 5D 6
Kentwood Cl. OX10: Chol 4D 42
Kestrels, The OX12: Gro 3E 45
Kew Win OX11: Did 1A 30
Kibble Cl. OX11: Did 3A 30
Kimber Rd. OX14: Abin 6G 5
Kimbers Cl. OX12: Den 1B 44
Kinecroft OX10: Wal 4G 33
King Alfred Dr. OX11: Did 2G 29
Kingfisher Cl. OX14: Abin 3B 10
Kingfishers OX12: Gro 5F 45
Kings Av. OX13: Marc 6A 4
Kings Cl. OX12: L Reg 5B 46
Kingsholme Cl.
  OX11: E Hag 6H 29
Kings La. OX11: Har 4A 28
King's Orchard
  OX10: B Sot 6C 22
Kingston Cl. OX14: Abin 5B 6
King Wlk. OX11: Did 1G 29
Kirby Cl. OX11: S Mor 6F 31
Knapp Cl. OX14: Abin 5H 5
Knolly's Cl. OX14: Abin 2C 6
Kynaston Rd. OX11: Did 3G 29
Kysbie Cl. OX14: Abin 3B 6

L

Laburnum Av. OX13: Ship 4G 5
  (not continuous)
Laburnum Gro. OX11: Did 3H 29
Ladycroft Cvn. Pk.
  OX11: Blew 4A 40
Lady Eleanor Ct.
  OX14: Abin 2H 9
Lady Gro. OX11: Did 4B 20
Ladygrove OX14: Abin 1H 9
Ladygrove Ct. OX14: Abin 1H 9
Lady Pl. OX14: S Cou 1C 18

Lake Rd. OX11: E Hag 5G 29
Lambe Av. OX14: Milt 6G 17
Lambrick Way OX14: Abin 3A 10
Lambwath Stream
  OX11: Did 6H 19
Lammas Cl. OX14: Abin 4B 6
Lancaster Av. OX10: Ben 6F 25
Landseer Wlk.
  OX14: Abin 2A 10
Lane, The OX11: Chil 5A 38
Lane End OX10: C Gif 4C 34
Langley Rd. OX14: Abin 3B 6
Lapwing La. OX10: Chol 4E 43
Larkdown OX12: Wan 3G 47
Larkfield OX10: Chol 4E 43
Lark Hill OX12: Wan 3G 47
Larkhill Pl. OX14: Abin 4H 5
Larkhill Rd. OX14: Abin 5A 6
Latton Cl. OX11: Chil 5A 38
Laurel Cres. OX12: Gro 5F 45
Lawson La. OX11: Chil 5H 37
Lay Av. OX10: Ber 1A 14
Leach Rd. OX10: Ber 2B 14
Lea Gro. OX11: Did 1H 29
Lee Av. OX14: Abin 5D 6
Lely Ct. OX14: Abin 2A 10
Lenthall Rd. OX14: Abin 5B 6
Lesparre Cl. OX14: Dray 5F 9
Lester Way OX10: Wal 4F 33
Letcombe Av. OX14: Abin 5A 6
Letcombe Hill
  OX12: E Cha 3B 46
LETCOMBE REGIS 5B 46
Letcombe Wlk. OX12: Gro 4E 45
Levery Cl. OX14: Abin 5E 7
Library Av. OX11: Har 3F 37
Liddiard Cl. OX12: Wan 1E 47
Lido Rd. OX11: Chil 5D 36
Limborough Rd.
  OX12: Wan 2E 47
  (not continuous)
Limes, The OX10: C Gif 4B 34
  OX10: D Tha 5B 14
Limetree Cl. OX12: Gro 4E 45
Limetrees OX11: Chil 4A 38
Linacre Cl. OX11: Did 3B 30
Lincoln Gdns. OX11: Did 3B 30
Linden Cres. OX12: Gro 4G 45
Linden Ga. OX11: Har 4A 28
Lindsay Dr. OX14: Abin 3D 6
Linnet Cl. OX14: Bur 3H 13
Lit. Howe Cl. OX14: Rad 2G 7
Little La. OX13: Stev 5D 16
Little Langlands
  OX11: E Hag 4H 29
LITTLE WITTENHAM 2G 21
Little Wittenham Nature Reserve
  ......3H 21
Lit. Wittenham Rd.
  OX14: Lit W, Lon W 6E 13
LITTLEWORTH 5A 24
Lit. Worth Hill
  OX12: Wan 2D 46
Littleworth Rd. OX10: Ben 5A 24
Lockinge Cl. OX11: Did 4G 29
Locks La. OX12: Wan 3D 46
Lockway OX14: Dray 1E 17
Lodden Av. OX10: Ber 2A 14
Loddon Cl. OX14: Abin 4D 6
Loddon Dr. OX11: Did 2B 30
Loder Rd. OX11: Har 4A 28
Lodge Hill Interchange
  OX13: Bay 1D 6
Lombard St. OX14: Abin 1B 10
London Rd.
  OX11: Blew, Upt, W Hag 6C 28
Longfellow Dr. OX14: Abin 2G 9
Longfields OX13: Marc 6B 4
Longford Way OX11: Did 1H 29
Long Furlong Rd.
  OX13: Spri 1H 5
Longmead OX14: Abin 4A 6
Long Tow OX13: Ship 3G 5

LONG WITTENHAM 1C 20
Long Wittenham Rd.
  OX11: N Mor 2F 31
Lostock Pl. OX11: Did 1H 29
Lovelace Cl. OX14: Abin 2C 6
Love La. OX10: Ewel 1H 35
LOWER RADLEY 3H 7
Lower Rd. OX11: Chil 5H 37
Lower Shrubbery
  OX14: Rad 2F 7
Lower Wharf OX10: Wal 4H 33
Loyd Cl. OX14: Abin 2C 6
Loyd Rd. OX11: Did 4F 29
Lucca Dr. OX14: Abin 3H 9
Lumberd Rd. OX14: Abin 3D 6
Lune Cl. OX11: Did 2A 30
Lupton Rd. OX10: Wal 4F 33
Lydalls Cl. OX11: Did 2F 29
Lydalls Rd. OX11: Did 2F 29
Lydsee Ga. OX12: Wan 2C 46
Lyford Cl. OX14: Dray 5F 9
Lyford Way OX14: Abin 3D 6
Lynch, The OX12: E Hen 6B 26
Lyndene Rd. OX11: Did 6F 19
Lynges Cl. OX14: Abin 3D 6
Lynmount Rd. OX11: Did 3G 29
Lyon Cl. OX14: Abin 4C 6

M

Maberley Cl. OX14: Abin 1G 9
Mably Gro. OX12: Wan 1E 47
Mably Way OX12: Wan 6D 44
Macdonald Cl. OX11: Did 2F 29
McKee Sq. OX10: Ben 1E 35
MACKNEY 3B 32
Mackney La. OX10: B Sot 1C 32
McMullan Cl. OX10: Wal 3G 33
Magdalen Ct. OX11: Did 3B 30
Magnette Cl. OX14: Abin 6B 6
Main Rd.
  OX11: Cos, E Hag 6F 29
  OX14: App 3H 19
Main St. OX11: Chil 5H 37
  OX11: W Hag 1E 39
  OX12: L Reg 6B 46
Mallard Way OX12: Gro 4E 45
Malthouse La.
  OX10: D Tha 6B 14
Malvern Cl. OX11: Did 1E 29
Mandarin Pl. OX12: Gro 4D 44
Mandeville Cl. OX14: Abin 3C 6
Mandhill Cl. OX12: Gro 5F 45
Mansfield Gdns. OX11: Did 3B 30
Manor Cl. OX11: Chil 4A 38
  OX11: W Hag 1E 39
  OX14: App 1H 19
  OX14: Dray 6F 9
Manor Ct. OX14: Abin 1A 10
Manor Cres. OX11: Did 3F 29
Mnr. Farm Rd.
  OX10: D Tha 6B 14
Manor Fld. OX12: L Reg 5B 46
Manor Grn. OX11: Har 4A 28
Manor La. OX12: W Hen 5A 26
Manor Rd. OX11: Did 2F 29
  OX12: Wan 6E 47
Maples, The OX12: Gro 3E 45
MARCHAM 1A 8
Marcham Rd. OX13: Marc 1C 8
  OX14: Abin 1F 9
  OX14: Dray 6E 9
Marcham Rd. Interchange
  OX13: Marc 1F 9
Maria Cres. OX12: Wan 2F 47
Marina Way OX14: Abin 3B 10
Mariot Ct. OX10: Wal 4H 33
Market Pl. OX10: Wal 4H 33
  (off St Martin's St.)
  OX11: Did 2H 29
  OX12: Wan 3E 47
  (not continuous)
  OX14: Abin 6B 6

Marlow Cl. OX10: Wal 3F **33**
Marnshey OX12: Wan 2D **46**
Marsh Ct. OX14: Abin 5B **6**
Marsh La. OX12: E Cha 5A **44**
Martin's La. OX10: D Tha . .5B **14**
Martyn's Way
  OX10: Ewel 5H **25**
Mayfield OX12: Wan 3F **47**
Marygreen OX12: Gro 5F **45**
Marymead OX10: Chol 3D **42**
Mary Whipple Ct.
  OX12: Wan 3D **46**
Masefield Cres.
  OX14: Abin 2G **9**
Mattock Way OX14: Abin . .2D **6**
Maud Ho. OX14: Abin 2G **47**
Maxwell Av. OX11: Har 2F **37**
Mayfield Av. OX12: Gro 5F **45**
Mayott's Rd. OX14: Abin . . .6A **6**
Meadow Cl. OX12: Gro 4F **45**
Meadow La. OX10: C Gif . . .5C **34**
Meadowside OX14: Abin . . .1A **10**
Meadowside Ct.
  *OX14: Abin 1A **10***
  (off Meadowside)
Meadow Way OX11: Did 4E **29**
Meads Cl. OX14: Dray 5F **9**
MEADSIDE 1C **22**
Mead Wlk. OX11: Did 1G **29**
Meashill Way OX11: Chil . . .5D **36**
Medina Cl. OX11: Did 2B **30**
Medlicott Dr. OX14: Abin . . .1G **9**
Medlock Gro. OX11: Did . . .6H **19**
Medway Cl. OX13: Ship 2G **5**
Medway Gro. OX11: Did . . .3A **30**
Medway Rd. OX13: Ship 2G **5**
Meer, The OX10: Ben 4C **24**
Melton Dr. OX11: Did 2G **29**
Membury Way
  OX12: Gro 5E **45**
Mendip Hgts. OX11: Did . . .1E **29**
Mere Dyke Rd.
  OX13: Stev 4D **16**
Mereland OX11: Did 4H **29**
Meriden Ct. OX10: Wal 4G **33**
Merlin Cl. OX10: Ben 1F **35**
  OX13: Abin 4F **5**
Merritt Rd. OX11: Did 2E **29**
Mersey Way OX11: Did 1A **30**
Merton Cl. OX11: Did 3B **30**
Metcalfe Cl. OX14: Abin . . .3A **10**
Mews, The OX10: Shil 4F **23**
Middle Furlong
  OX11: Did 1B **30**
Midget Cl. OX14: Abin 2H **9**
Midwinter Av.
  OX14: Milt 6G **17**
Miles Dr. OX12: Gro 5F **45**
Millbrook Cl. OX10: Wal . . .4G **33**
  OX11: Blew 4A **40**
Millham, The
  OX12: W Hen 5A **26**
Millington Rd. OX10: Wal . .3G **33**
Mill La. OX10: Ben 5B **24**
  OX10: Wal 4H **33**
  OX11: S Mor 6F **31**
  OX12: Gro 5F **45**
  OX12: W Hen 5A **26**
  (not continuous)
  OX14: Milt 3G **17**
  OX14: S Cou 1B **18**
Mill Paddock
  OX12: L Reg 5B **46**
  OX14: Abin 1B **10**
Mill Rd. OX13: Marc 2B **8**
  OX14: Abin 2G **9**
Mill Stream Ct.
  OX14: Abin 1B **10**
Mill St. OX12: Wan 2D **46**
  OX13: Stev 6D **16**
MILTON 4H **17**
Milton Bus. and Technology Cen.
  OX13: M Hil 2E **27**
MILTON HEIGHTS 6G **17**

MILTON HILL 2F **27**
Milton Hill OX13: M Hil . . .2F **27**
Milton Interchange
  OX14: Stev 6G **17**
Milton La. OX13: Stev 4E **17**
  (not continuous)
  OX14: Stev 4E **17**
Milton Manor 4G **17**
Milton Pk. Est. OX14: Milt . .5A **18**
  (not continuous)
Milton Rd OX11: Did 6B **18**
  OX14: Dray, S Cou 6H **9**
  OX14: Milt 6B **18**
  OX14: S Cou 3A **18**
Minchins Cl. OX14: Abin . . .5E **7**
Minns Rd. OX12: Gro 4G **45**
Moir Ct. OX12: Wan 2E **47**
Monarchs Ct. OX10: Ben . . .5B **24**
MONGEWELL 1H **43**
Monks Cl. OX10: D Tha 6C **14**
Monks Lode OX11: Did 6H **19**
Monks Mead OX10: B Sot . .1C **32**
Mons Way OX14: Abin 5H **5**
Moorbrook OX11: Did 5F **19**
Moorlands, The
  OX14: Abin 5B **24**
Moreton Av. OX10: Wal 4F **33**
Moreton Rd.
  OX11: A Tir, A Upt 4F **41**
Morland Rd. OX13: Marc . . .1B **8**
Morrells Cl. OX11: Did 2F **29**
Morse Rd. OX11: Did 5F **29**
Morton Cl. OX14: Abin 5D **6**
Mosquito La. OX11: Ben . . .1F **35**
Motte, The OX14: Abin 5B **6**
Mousey La. *OX10: Wal 4H **33***
  (off Wood St.)
Mowbray Rd.
  OX11: Did 5G **29**
Mullard Way OX14: Abin . . .6A **6**
Murren, The OX10: Wal 5H **33**
Murren Cft. OX10: C Gif . . .4A **34**
Musson Cl. OX14: Abin 1A **10**

N

Naldertown OX12: Wan 2C **46**
Napier Ct. OX14: Abin 6D **6**
Nash Dr. OX14: Abin 1G **9**
Neave M. OX14: Abin 1B **10**
Nelson Cl. OX10: Wal 3G **33**
Nene Gro. OX11: Did 1B **30**
Nene Rd. OX13: Ship 3G **5**
Newbury Rd.
  OX12: E Hen 6B **26**
Newbury St. OX12: Wan . . .3E **47**
NEWINGTON 2H **15**
Newlands Dr. OX12: Gro . . .5D **44**
Newlands Rd.
  OX11: Did 4G **29**
Newman La. OX14: Dray 5F **9**
Newmans Cl. OX11: Upt . . .2E **39**
Newnham Grn.
  OX10: C Gif 4A **34**
  (not continuous)
New Rd. OX10: Shil 3F **23**
  OX10: Wal 4H **33**
  OX11: E Hag 5A **30**
  OX14: Rad 3G **7**
New St. OX10: Ben 6B **6**
Newton Way OX10: Ben 4C **24**
Nicholson Ho. OX14: Abin . .2H **9**
Nineteenth St.
  OX11: Har 3D **36**
Ninth St. OX11: Har 2F **37**
Nobles Cl. OX12: Gro 4E **45**
Nor Brook Cl. OX14: Abin . . .3E **7**
Norfolk Cl. OX14: Rad 3G **7**
Norman Av. OX14: Abin 4C **6**
Norman Way OX10: Wal . . .4G **33**
Norreys Cl. OX11: Did 4F **29**
Norreys Rd. OX11: Did 3F **29**
Norries Dr. OX10: Wal 2H **33**

Norris Cl. OX14: Abin 3D **6**
North Av. OX14: Abin 3C **6**
Nth. Bush Furlong
  OX11: Did 2B **30**
NORTHCOURT 3D **6**
Northcourt La. OX14: Abin . .4C **6**
Northcourt Rd.
  OX14: Abin 4A **6**
Northcourt Wlk.
  OX14: Abin 5C **6**
North Cft. OX11: E Hag 6H **29**
North Dr. OX11: Har 1G **37**
  OX12: Gro 3F **45**
Northfield Rd. OX14: Abin . . .2C **6**
NORTH MORETON 3G **31**
North Quay OX14: Abin 3B **10**
North Rd. OX11: Did 1E **29**
NORTH STOKE 4H **43**
North Way OX13: Stev 5D **16**
Nosworthy Rd.
  OX10: C Gif, Wal 6H **33**
Nuffield Cl. OX11: Did 3A **30**
Nuffield La. OX10: Ben 5F **35**
Nuffield Way OX14: Abin . . .6G **5**
Nuneham Sq.
  OX14: Abin 5A **6**
Nunney Brook OX11: Did . . .6H **19**
Nursery, The
  OX14: S Cou 1B **18**
Nyatt Rd. OX14: Abin 5E **7**

O

Oakley Ct. OX10: Ben 6H **35**
Oakley Pk. OX13: F Hea 3A **4**
Oatland Rd. OX11: Did 3G **29**
Oatlands Cl. OX10: War 2F **23**
Observatory Cl.
  OX10: Ben 5C **24**
Ock Dr. OX10: Ber 2B **14**
Ockley Brook OX11: Did . . .1A **30**
Ock M. OX14: Abin 6A **6**
Ock Mill Cl. OX14: Abin 1H **9**
Ock St. OX14: Abin 1H **9**
Offas Cl. OX10: Ben 4C **24**
Ogbourne Cl. OX12: Wan . . .2C **46**
Old Barn Cl. OX10: Ben 5C **24**
Old Blackalls Dr.
  OX10: Chol 2E **43**
Old Bourne OX11: Did 6G **19**
Old Farm Cl. OX14: Abin . . .5E **7**
Old Gaol (Sports & Arts Cen.)
  . . . . .1B **10**
  (off Bridge St.)
Old London Rd.
  OX10: Ben 5C **24**
Old Manor Ct.
  OX12: L Reg 5B **46**
Old Man's La. OX12: Gro . . .1H **45**
Old Mill Cl. OX12: Gro 4F **45**
Old Moor OX14: Milt 4H **17**
Old Moor Cl. OX10: Wal . . .4G **33**
Old Reading Rd.
  OX10: C Gif 4B **34**
Old Rd. OX12: E Hen 5C **26**
Old School La.
  OX12: E Cha 2A **46**
Old Stables Yd.
  OX12: L Reg 6B **46**
Old Station Yd. OX14: Abin . .6B **6**
Old Wallingford Way
  OX14: S Cou 1C **18**
Omega Pk. OX11: Did 6G **19**
One End Cl. OX10: Ben 5B **24**
Orchard, The OX12: E Cha . .2B **46**
Orchard Cl. OX10: Shil 2F **23**
  OX10: Wal 5H **33**
  OX11: Did 2G **29**
  OX11: Upt 3E **39**
  OX12: E Hen 4B **26**
  OX14: Abin 4C **6**
Orchard Haven
  OX10: D Tha 1B **22**

Orchard La. OX12: E Hen . . .5B **26**
Orchard Way OX11: Har 4H **27**
  OX12: Wan 3F **47**
  OX13: Marc 1B **8**
Orchids, The OX11: Chil 6H **37**
Ordnance Rd. OX11: Did . . .1F **29**
  (not continuous)
Oriel Ct. OX11: Did 3B **30**
Ormond Rd. OX12: Wan . . .3E **47**
Orpwood Way OX14: Abin . . .1G **9**
Orwell Dr. OX11: Did 2A **30**
Osiers, The OX10: D Leo . . .1F **15**
Ottery Way OX11: Did 1A **30**
Otwell Cl. OX14: Abin 3D **6**
Ouse Cl. OX11: Did 6H **19**
Oval, The OX11: Did 1E **29**
Overmead OX14: Abin 3H **9**
OVERY 1C **22**
Oxford Cres. OX11: Did 3E **29**
Oxford La. OX12: Gro 3F **45**
Oxford Rd. OX10: Ben 5A **24**
  OX10: D Tha 4B **14**
  OX14: Abin 5C **6**
  OX14: C Ham 3D **12**
  OX44: N Cou 3D **12**

P

Packhorse La.
  OX13: Marc 1B **8**
Paddock OX14: Abin 1H **9**
Paddock, The OX11: Chil . . .5H **37**
Paddock Cl. OX10: Ben 5C **24**
  OX12: Wan 1G **47**
Paddock Rd. OX10: Wal 5H **33**
Page Furlong
  OX10: D Tha 5B **14**
Pagisters Rd. OX14: Abin . . .3E **7**
Pain Way OX10: War 5E **15**
Palmer Pl. OX14: Abin 2A **10**
Palmers Rd. OX12: Wan . . .2G **47**
Panters Rd. OX10: Chol 4D **42**
Paper Mill La.
  OX11: S Mor 6G **31**
Papist Way OX10: Chol 4D **42**
Park, The OX11: Har 5A **28**
Park 34 OX11: Did 5G **19**
Park Cl. OX11: Did 3F **29**
Park Rd. OX11: Did 6F **29**
  OX14: Abin 6H **5**
Park Side OX13: Marc 1A **8**
Park Ter. OX12: E Cha 2A **46**
Park Vw. OX10: C Gif 5C **34**
  OX12: Wan 2F **47**
Parsonage Cl. OX12: Wan . .1H **47**
Parsonage Moor Nature Reserve
  . . . . .1B **4**
Parson's La. OX10: Ewel . . .5G **25**
Parsons Mead OX14: Abin . . .4A **6**
Partridge Cl. OX12: Wan . . .3F **47**
Passey Cres. OX10: Ben 5C **24**
Paternoster La.
  OX10: Chol 4D **42**
Peachcroft Cen.
  OX14: Abin 3D **6**
Peachcroft Rd. OX14: Abin . .3D **6**
Peacock Ho. *OX12: Wan . . .3E **47***
  (off Post Office La.)
Peat Moor La. OX13: Marc . .6D **4**
Peeble Dr. OX11: Did 4A **30**
Peep-O-Day La.
  OX14: Abin 5A **10**
Pembroke Cl. OX14: Milt . . .4G **17**
Pendon Mus. 1C **20**
Pen La. OX13: Spri 1B **6**
  OX14: Abin 1B **6**
Penn Cl. OX14: Abin 3E **7**
Pennygreen La.
  OX10: B Sot 1C **32**
Penpont Water OX11: Did . .1A **30**
Pensfield OX10: Ben 5A **24**
Pentagon, The OX14: Abin . . .6D **6**

Peregrine Way OX12: Gro 4E 45
Perimeter Rd. OX11: Chil . . .3G 37
Phyllis Chiltern Mus. 4H 33
(off St Peter's Pl.)
Picklers Hill OX14: Abin 3C 6
Pixton Cl. OX11: Did 3F 29
Plantation Rd. OX11: Chil 5D 36
Plough Cl. OX10: Shil 3F 23
Plumbe Ct. OX12: Wan 1E 47
Pluto Rd. OX11: Chil 5D 36
Plym Dr. OX11: Did 1A 30
Pollocks La. OX10: N Sto 4H 43
Port Hill Rd. OX10: Ben 4B 24
Port Way OX10: C Gif 6B 34
OX12: Wan, W Loc 2H 47
Portway OX11: Did 4E 29
OX12: Wan 3E 47
Portway M. OX12: Wan 3E 47
Post Office La.
OX12: L Reg 6B 46
OX12: Wan 3E 47
Potenger Way OX14: Abin 1H 9
Potters La. OX10: Ewel 1H 35
Pound, The OX10: Chol 3D 42
OX12: Wan 2H 47
Pound Cft. OX12: Gro 5E 45
Pound La. OX10: Chol 3D 42
OX11: Upt 3E 39
PRESTON CROWMARSH . . .6B 24
Preston Rd. OX14: Abin 2H 9
Prestwick Burn OX11: Did . . .6H 19
Priest's Moor La.
OX10: War 6D 14
Prince Gro. OX14: Abin 2B 6
Princess Gdns.
OX12: Gro 5D 44
Priory La. OX13: Marc 1B 8
Priory Orchard
OX12: Wan 2D 46
Priory Rd. OX12: Wan 3E 47
Pritchard Cl. OX10: Ber 1A 14
Prospect Rd. OX11: Upt 3E 39
Pudsey Cl. OX14: Abin 3A 10
Pugsden La. OX13: Stev 5E 17
Puma Cl. OX10: Ben 1F 35
Purslane OX14: Abin 5D 6
Pykes Cl. OX14: Abin 3D 6
Pytenry Cl. OX14: Abin 2D 6

Q

Quadrant, The OX14: Abin . . .6D 6
Quaker La. OX10: War 1F 23
Quantock Vw. OX11: Did 1E 29
Queen Elizabeth Cl.
OX11: Did 3A 30
Queen's Av. OX10: Wal 2F 33
Queens Cl. OX10: D Tha 6B 14
Queens Rd. OX10: Chol 4D 42
Queen St. OX10: D Tha 6B 14
OX14: Abin 6B 6
Queens Way OX10: Ben 6F 25
OX11: N Mor 3F 31
Queensway OX11: Did 4F 29

R

RADLEY 3G 7
Radley Rd. OX14: Abin 5C 6
Radley Rd. Ind. Est.
OX14: Abin 4D 6
Radley Station (Rail) 3H 7
Radnor Rd. OX10: Wal 3F 33
Rainbow Way OX14: Abin 2D 6
Ramsons Way OX14: Abin 5E 7
Rawlins Gro. OX14: Abin 5H 5
Rawthey Av. OX11: Did 5H 19
Ray Cl. OX11: Did 1A 30
Reade Av. OX14: Abin 5D 6
Reading Rd.
OX10: Chol, Moul, Wal
. . . . .6E 43

Reading Rd. OX10: Wal 5H 33
OX11: Har 4G 27
Rectory La. OX11: A Tir 4F 41
Reeds Cl. OX12: Wan 2E 47
Regent Cinema 3E 47
(within Regent Shop. Mall)
Regent Gdns. OX11: Did 3B 30
Regent Shop. Mall, The
OX12: Wan 3E 47
(off Newbury St.)
Regis Pl. OX12: L Reg 5B 46
Retreat Gdns. OX10: C Gif . . .4A 34
Reynolds Way
OX12: E Cha 2A 46
OX14: Abin 2A 10
Richmere Rd. OX11: Did 4H 29
Ridge Way OX12: Wan 5B 44
Ridgeway Rd. OX11: Did 4H 29
Riley Cl. OX14: Abin 1H 9
River Cl. OX14: Abin 2A 10
Riverside Pk. & Pools 3A 34
River Vw. OX10: S Hil 5F 23
River Vw. Ter. OX14: Abin . . .1A 10
Rivy Cl. OX14: Abin 5E 7
Road One OX11: Chil 4E 37
Road Two OX11: Chil 4E 37
Road Four OX11: Chil 4E 37
Road Five OX11: Chil 4F 37
Road Six OX11: Chil 4F 37
Road Eight OX11: Chil 4E 37
Road Nine OX11: Chil 4F 37
Road Eleven OX11: Chil 4E 37
Road Twelve OX11: Chil 4E 37
Road Thirteen OX11: Chil 4F 37
Road Fifteen OX11: Chil 4E 37
Road Eighteen OX11: Chil 4F 37
Robert Sparrow Gdns.
OX10: C Gif 5C 34
Robinson Cl. OX11: Blew 5A 40
Roding Way OX11: Did 1A 30
Roebuck Ct. OX11: Did 3A 30
Roentgen Av. OX11: Har 3E 37
ROKE 2D 24
ROKERMARSH 3B 24
Rolls Ct. OX12: Wan 2E 47
Roman Pl. OX11: Did 1F 29
Roman Way OX12: Wan 1D 46
Rookery Cl. OX13: Ship 4F 5
Rose Av. OX14: Abin 2B 6
Rosebay Cres. OX12: Gro 5E 45
Rose Ter. OX12: Den 1B 44
Rother Gth. OX11: Did 6A 20
Rothwells Cl. OX10: Chol 3E 43
Rotten Row OX10: D Tha 6B 14
Rowans, The OX10: Chol 4C 42
Rowland Cl. OX10: Wal 2G 33
Rowland Rd. OX10: Chol 4E 43
Row Leigh La.
OX13: Bes, F Hea 1A 4
ROWSTOCK 4F 27
Roxburgh Dr. OX11: Did 6F 19
Royal Berkshire Ct.
OX11: Did 4H 29
Rugge Furlong OX11: Did 2B 30
Rumbolds Cl. OX10: Ben 4B 24
Rumbolds La.
OX49: B Bal 1G 25
Rumsey's La. OX11: Blew 5A 40
Rushmead Copse
OX14: Abin 3E 7
Ruskin Av. OX14: Abin 2A 10
Ruskin Cl. OX11: Did 3A 30
Russell Jackson Cl.
OX10: Ber 1A 14
Rutherford Av. OX11: Har 3E 37
Rutherford Cl. OX14: Abin 4C 6
Rymans Cres.
OX11: E Hag 5A 30

S

Saffron Ct. OX14: Abin 5D 6
St Alban's Ct. OX10: Wal 4H 33

St Amand Dr. OX14: Abin 1A 10
St Andrews Cl. OX14: Abin . . .3E 7
St Andrew's Rd.
OX11: Did 3H 29
St Annes Ct. OX11: Did 4B 30
St Edmund's La.
OX14: Abin 1B 10
St George's Cl.
OX10: Chol 4D 42
St Georges Grn.
OX10: Wal 2G 33
St Georges Rd.
OX10: Wal 3G 33
St Helen's Av. OX10: Ben . . .6B 24
St Helen's Ct. OX14: Abin . . .1B 10
St Helen's Cres.
OX10: Ben 6B 24
St Helens M. OX14: Abin . . .1B 10
(off East St Helen St.)
St Helen's Wharf
OX14: Abin 1B 10
St Hildas Cl. OX11: Did 4B 30
St Hughs Ri. OX11: Did 4B 30
St Ives La. OX12: Gro 5F 45
(off Main St.)
St Ives Rd. OX12: Gro 5F 45
St James OX12: Wan 1E 47
St James Rd. OX14: Rad 2G 7
St John's Cl. OX11: Did 3A 30
St Johns Ct. OX12: Gro 4F 45
St John's Grn.
OX10: Wal 4H 33
St John's Rd. OX10: Wal 4G 33
OX12: Gro 4F 45
OX14: Abin 5C 6
St John's Row
OX14: Lon W 1C 20
St John's Ter. OX10: Wal 4G 33
St Lawrence Cl.
OX10: War 1F 23
St Lawrence Ho.
OX10: War 1F 23
(off St Lawrence Cl.)
St Leonard's Ct.
OX10: Wal 5H 33
St Leonard's La.
OX10: Wal 4H 33
St Leonard's Sq.
OX10: Wal 4H 33
St Lucian's La.
OX10: Wal 5H 33
St Martin's St. OX10: Wal . . .4H 33
St Mary's Grn. OX14: Abin . . .4A 6
St Mary's Rd.
OX12: E Hen 5C 26
St Mary's St. OX10: Wal 4H 33
St Mary's Way
OX12: Wan 1D 46
St Michael's Av.
OX14: Abin 6A 6
St Michael's Way
OX13: Stev 5D 16
St Nicholas' Grn.
OX14: Abin 4A 6
St Nicholas Pl.
OX12: E Cha 2A 46
St Nicholas Rd.
OX10: Wal 3G 33
St Peter's Pl. OX10: Wal 4H 33
St Peter's Rd. OX11: Did 3G 29
OX14: Abin 4E 7
St Peter's St. OX10: Wal 4H 33
St Ruald's Cl. OX10: Wal 4H 33
St Rumbold's Rd.
OX10: Wal 4G 33
Samian Way OX10: D Tha . . .1B 22
Samor Way OX11: Did 3F 29
Sandford Cl. OX14: Abin 3D 6
Sandringham Rd.
OX11: Did 3A 30
Sands, The
OX10: Ben, Rok 4C 24
OX10: Rok 3F 25
Sands Rd. OX11: S Mor 5F 31

Sands Way OX10: Ben 4B 24
Sandy La. OX10: Chol 4C 42
Sarajac Av. OX12: E Cha 3A 46
Savile Way OX12: Gro 4D 44
Saxon Cl. OX10: Wal 4G 33
Saxon Ct. OX10: Ben 5B 24
Saxon Pl. OX12: Wan 2C 46
Saxons Heath
OX14: Lon W 2D 20
Saxons Way OX11: Did 4A 30
Saxton Rd. OX14: Abin 2H 9
Sayers Orchard OX11: Did . . .2F 29
Schongau Cl. OX14: Abin 3H 9
School Cl. OX13: Stev 5D 16
School La. OX11: Har 4A 28
OX12: Gro 4E 45
OX14: App 1H 19
OX14: Milt 6G 17
(not continuous)
Science Pk. OX14: Abin 6D 6
Second Av. OX11: Did 1F 29
Second St. OX11: Har 2G 37
Seesen Way OX12: Wan 2F 47
Segsbury Ct. OX12: Wan 2C 46
Segsbury Rd. OX12: Wan 2C 46
Sellwood Rd. OX14: Abin 3B 6
Selwyn Cres. OX14: Rad 3G 7
Seventeenth St.
OX11: Har 3E 37
Severalls Cl. OX10: Wal 2H 33
Severn Cres. OX11: Did 3A 30
Severn Rd. OX11: Chil 4F 37
OX13: Ship 3H 5
Sewell Cl. OX14: Abin 4E 7
Shadwell Rd. OX10: Ber 2H 13
Shannon Cl. OX12: Gro 4G 45
Shannon Rd. OX11: Did 3A 30
Sharland Cl. OX12: Gro 5E 45
Shaw's Copse OX14: Rad 3H 7
Sheepstead Rd.
OX13: Marc 5A 4
Sheepwash La.
OX13: Stev 4E 17
Shelley Cl. OX14: Abin 4C 6
Shepherd Gdns.
OX14: Abin 1G 9
Shepherds Cl. OX12: Gro 3E 45
Sherwood Av. OX14: Abin 6C 6
Sherwood Rd. OX11: Did 2F 29
SHILLINGFORD 3F 23
Shillingford Ct.
OX10: Shil 4E 23
SHILLINGFORD HILL 5F 23
Shinmoor Cl. OX11: Did 1B 30
SHIPPON 4G 5
Shoe La. OX11: E Hag 6H 29
(off Up. Cross La.)
Short Furlong OX11: Did 1B 30
Shrieves Cl. OX14: Abin 2D 6
(off Bucklers Bury Rd.)
Sidings, The OX10: Wal 4F 33
Simmonds Wlk.
OX12: Wan 1E 47
(off Witan Way)
Sinodun Cl. OX14: Lon W . . .2D 20
Sinodun Dr. OX10: Wal 2F 33
Sinodun Rd. OX11: Did 4H 29
Sinodun Vw. OX10: War 1F 23
Sint Niklaas Cl.
OX14: Abin 3H 9
Sires Hill OX10: B Sot 4F 21
OX11: N Mor 4F 21
OX14: Lon W 4C 20
Sixteenth St. OX11: Har 2F 37
Sixth St. OX11: Har 2F 37
SLADE END 1E 33
Slade End Rdbt.
OX10: B Sot 1E 33
Slade Rd. OX10: Chol 3E 43
OX11: Did 3E 29
Smiths Farm La.
OX11: Did 2F 29
Smiths Rickyard
OX12: E Hen 4B 26

Smiths Wharf OX12: Wan . . .2E **47**
Somerville OX11: Did 3B **30**
Sotwell St. OX10: B Sot 1C **32**
South Av. OX14: Abin 3B **6**
South Dr. OX11: Har 2G **37**
Southfield Dr.
   OX14: S Cou 2B **18**
Southmead Ind. Est.
   OX11: Did 5F **19**
Southmoor Way
   OX14: Abin 5A **6**
SOUTH MORETON **6F 31**
South Pk. Av. OX11: Did . . .4F **29**
South Quay OX14: Abin 3B **10**
South St. OX11: Blew 5A **40**
   OX12: L Reg 6B **46**
South Vw. OX10: Wal 4G **33**
   (off Croft Rd.)
   OX11: Chil 5H **37**
Sovereign Cl. OX11: Did . . .3A **30**
Sovereign Pl. OX10: Wal . . .5G **33**
Spenlove Cl. OX14: Abin 3B **6**
Spey Rd. OX13: Ship 2G **5**
Spinney, The OX12: E Hen . .5B **26**
   OX14: Abin 4H **5**
Spinneys Cl. OX14: Rad 2H **7**
Spitfire Cl. OX10: Ben 1D **34**
Springdale OX10: Wal 4G **33**
Springfield Dr. OX14: Abin . . .5A **6**
Springfield Rd.
   OX12: Wan 3F **47**
Spring Gdns. OX14: Abin . . .6H **5**
Spring La.
   OX11: A Tir, A Upt 5E **41**
Spring Rd. OX14: Abin 6H **5**
Springs Hotel & Golf Club, The
   . . . . .4H **43**
Spring Ter. OX14: Abin 6H **5**
   (off Spring Rd.)
Squires Ho. OX12: Wan 2E **47**
   (off Smiths Wharf)
Squire's Wlk. OX10: Wal . . .5H **33**
Stadhampton Rd.
   OX10: D Leo 2F **15**
Stanford Dr. OX14: Abin 6B **6**
Staniland Ct. OX14: Abin 5B **6**
Star Ter. OX12: Den 1B **44**
Station Rd. OX10: Chol 4D **42**
   OX10: Wal 3F **33**
   OX11: Did 1G **29**
   OX11: Upt 3E **39**
   OX12: Gro 5F **45**
   OX14: Cul 4H **11**
Station Rd. Ind. Est.
   OX10: Wal 3G **33**
Station Yd. OX13: Stev 5E **17**
Stenton Cl. OX14: Abin 2A **10**
Steptoe Cl. OX12: Gro 3E **45**
Stert St. OX14: Abin 6B **6**
Stevenson Dr. OX14: Abin . . .5H **5**
STEVENTON **5E 17**
Steventon Rd. OX14: Dray . . .3E **17**
   (not continuous)
Steventon Storage Facility
   OX13: Stev 4A **16**
Stileway Rd.
   OX11: Chil, Har 5D **36**
   OX12: E Hen 5D **36**
Stirling Cl. OX12: Wan 2F **47**
Stirlings Rd. OX12: Wan 2E **47**
Stockey End OX14: Abin 3E **7**
Stockham Pk. OX12: Wan . . .1D **46**
Stockham Way
   OX12: Wan 2D **46**
Stocks La. OX13: Stev 5D **16**
Stonebridge La.
   OX13: Stev 4D **16**
Stonebury Cl. OX12: Wan . . .2F **47**
Stonehill La. OX14: Dray 3G **9**
Stonehill Wlk. OX14: Abin . . .3H **9**
   (off Kensington Cl.)
Stonesfield OX11: Did 4A **30**
Stonhouse Cres.
   OX14: Rad 3G **7**

Stonor Cl. OX11: Did 2G **29**
Stort Cl. OX11: Did 6H **19**
Stour Cl. OX11: Did 2A **30**
Stratton Way OX14: Abin 6B **6**
Stream Rd. OX11: Upt 3E **39**
Street, The OX10: C Gif 4A **34**
   OX10: N Sto 4H **43**
Styles, The OX11: Har 4H **27**
Suffolk Way OX14: Abin 1H **9**
Summer Flds. OX14: Abin 2D **6**
Sunningwell Rd.
   OX13: Spri 2H **5**
Sunnyside OX10: Ben 4B **24**
Sutherland Beck
   OX11: Did 6G **19**
Sutton Cl. OX14: Abin 6B **6**
SUTTON COURTENAY **2C 18**
Sutton Courtenay Rd.
   OX14: Milt 5B **18**
Sutton Rd. OX14: Milt 3H **17**
SUTTON WICK **5F 9**
Sutton Wick La.
   OX14: Dray 5F **9**
Suzan Cres. OX12: Wan 2F **47**
Swale Dr. OX11: Did 1A **30**
Swan Cl. OX12: Gro 4D **44**
Swarbourne Cl.
   OX11: Did 1H **29**
Sweet Briar OX13: Marc 1B **8**
Swift Way OX10: Ben 6F **25**
Swinburne Rd.
   OX14: Abin 5C **6**
Sycamore Cl. OX13: Abin . . .4F **5**
Sycamore Wlk.
   OX12: Gro 4E **45**
Sympson Cl. OX14: Abin 1A **10**
Synderford Cl. OX11: Did . . .1A **30**

T

Tamar Way OX11: Did 1A **30**
Tanners Row OX12: Wan 2E **47**
   (off Smiths Wharf)
Tarret Burn OX11: Did 6G **19**
Tatham Rd. OX14: Abin 4B **6**
Tatlings Rd. OX13: Stev 4D **16**
Tavistock Av. OX11: Did 4F **29**
Tavy Cl. OX11: Did 6H **19**
Teal Cl. OX12: Gro 4E **45**
Teescroft OX11: Did 6A **20**
Tennyson Dr. OX14: Abin 2G **9**
Tenpenny OX10: D Tha 1B **22**
Tenth St. OX11: Har 2F **37**
Terrington Cl. OX14: Abin . . .3C **6**
Thame La. OX14: Cul 4E **11**
Thame La. OX44: N Cou 4E **11**
Thame Rd. OX10: War 6F **15**
Thames Ct. OX11: Did 3A **30**
Thames Ct. OX14: Abin 6C **6**
Thames Mead
   OX10: C Gif 4A **34**
Thames Rd. OX11: Har 2E **37**
Thames St. OX10: Wal 4H **33**
   OX14: Abin 1B **10**
Thames Vw. OX14: Abin 6C **6**
Thames Vw. Ind. Pk.
   OX14: Abin 6C **6**
The . . . .
   Names prefixed with 'The' for
   example 'The Avenue' are
   indexed under the main name
   such as 'Avenue, The'
Thesiger Rd. OX14: Abin 5B **6**
Third St. OX11: Har 3F **37**
Thirteenth St. OX11: Har 3E **37**
Thistlecroft Cl. OX14: Abin . . .3D **6**
Thompson Av. OX11: Har 2F **37**
Thornhill Cl. OX12: Wan 2E **47**
Thornhill Wlk. OX14: Abin . . .4A **6**
Thorningdown OX11: Chil . . .5H **37**
Thorpe St. OX11: A Upt 4E **41**
Three Pigeons Cl.
   OX12: Wan 3F **47**

Three Poplar Mobile Home Pk.
   OX14: Lon W 1C **20**
Thrupp La. OX14: Rad 3F **7**
Thurne Vw. OX11: Did 2A **30**
Thurston Cl. OX14: Abin 1A **10**
Tiburn Glen OX11: Did 1H **29**
Tilsley Pk. (Sports Pk.) **2A 6**
Tinkerbush La.
   OX12: Wan 1E **47**
Tirrold Way OX12: Wan 2G **47**
Tollgate Rd. OX14: Cul 5D **10**
Torridge Dr. OX11: Did 1A **30**
Tourist Info. Cen.
   Abingdon **1B 10**
   Didcot **2H 29**
   Wallingford **4H 33**
   (within Town Hall)
Tower Cl. OX13: Marc 1B **8**
   OX14: Abin 1H **9**
Tower Gdns. OX11: Did 1E **29**
Tower Rd. OX10: Ben 1B **14**
Town Cl. OX14: S Cou 2C **18**
TOWNSEND **3C 46**
Townsend OX11: Chil 4H **37**
   OX11: Har 3A **28**
   OX14: Abin 1A **10**
Trenchard Av. OX14: Milt 6G **17**
Trenchard Cl. OX10: Wal 4G **33**
Trent Rd. OX11: Did 1A **30**
Trinder Rd. OX12: Wan 3F **47**
Trinity Cl. OX14: Abin 3D **6**
Truelocks Way
   OX12: Wan 1G **47**
Tubbs Cl. OX12: Gro 5E **45**
Tudor Cl. OX10: Wal 4G **33**
Tullis Cl. OX14: S Cou 2B **18**
Tulwick La. OX12: Gro 3G **45**
Turberville Cl.
   OX14: Abin 1A **10**
Turnagain La. OX14: Abin . . .1B **10**
Turner Rd. OX14: Abin 2H **9**
Turners Cl. OX14: Rad 3H **7**
Tweed Dr. OX11: Did 5H **19**
Twelfth St. OX11: Har 2F **37**
Twelve Acre Dr.
   OX14: Abin 2D **6**
Twentieth St. OX11: Har 3D **36**
Tyne Av. OX11: Did 1H **29**
Tyne Rd. OX13: Ship 3G **5**
Tyne St. OX11: Did 3A **30**
Tyrrells Cl. OX11: Har 5H **27**
Tyrrell's Way
   OX14: S Cou 3A **18**

U

Unicorn Theatre **6C 6**
Up. Cross La.
   OX11: E Hag 6H **29**
Upperway Furlong
   OX11: Did 1B **30**
Upthorpe Dr. OX12: Wan 1F **47**
UPTON **3E 39**
Upton Cl. OX14: Abin 4C **6**
Usk Way OX11: Did 6A **20**

V

Vale & Downland Mus. & Vis Cen.
   . . . .**3E 47**
Vale Av. OX12: Gro 4F **45**
Vale Rd. OX11: Har 2F **37**
Valetta Way OX10: Ben 6F **25**
Vauxhall Way OX11: Did 1F **29**
Venners Water OX11: Did . . .6A **20**
Verlam Gro. OX11: Did 1B **30**
Vestry Cl. OX12: Gro 3E **45**
Vicarage Cl. OX12: Gro 4F **45**
Vicarage Hill OX12: E Cha . . .3B **46**
Vicarage Rd. OX11: Did 3H **29**
   OX13: Stev 5C **16**
Victoria Rd. OX14: Abin 6H **5**

Viking Dr. OX11: Did 4A **30**
Viking Ter. OX10: Ben 6F **25**
Villeboys Cl. OX14: Abin 5E **7**
Vineyard OX14: Abin 6B **6**
Virginia Way OX14: Abin 3H **9**

W

Wallace Cl. OX14: Abin 2A **10**
Walled Gdns. OX14: Rad 2G **7**
WALLINGFORD **4H 33**
WALLINGFORD COMMUNITY
   HOSPITAL **5G 33**
Wallingford Mus. **3G 33**
Wallingford Rd.
   OX10: Chol, Wal 3D **42**
   OX10: Mon, N Sto 6H **43**
   OX10: Shil 4F **23**
   OX11: N Mor 3G **31**
Wallingford Station
   Cholsey and
   Wallingford Railway
   . . . .**4F 33**
Wallingford St.
   OX12: Wan 3E **47**
Walter Bigg Way
   OX10: Wal 3G **33**
Wandle Beck OX11: Did 6H **19**
Wansbeck Wood
   OX11: Did 6A **20**
WANTAGE **3E 47**
WANTAGE HOSPITAL **2F 47**
Wantage Leisure Cen. **3E 47**
Wantage Rd. OX10: Wal 2E **33**
   OX11: Did 3E **29**
   OX11: Har 5H **27**
WARBOROUGH **1F 23**
Warborough Rd.
   OX10: Shil 3F **23**
   OX12: L Reg 6B **46**
Warmans Cl. OX12: Wan 2C **46**
Warner Cres. OX11: Did 4F **29**
Warwick Cl. OX14: Abin 5C **6**
Wasbrough Av.
   OX12: Wan 2D **46**
Washford Glen OX11: Did . . .1A **30**
Water La. OX10: D Leo 2F **15**
Waterman's La.
   OX10: B Sot 6B **22**
Watery La. OX14: C Ham 3D **12**
Watery La. Path
   OX10: C Gif 4A **34**
Watling La. OX10: D Tha 6B **14**
Watlington Rd.
   OX10: Ben 5B **24**
Watts La. OX11: Blew 5A **40**
Waveney Cl. OX11: Did 2A **30**
Waxes Cl. OX14: Abin 3E **7**
Wayland Av. OX12: Wan 5B **44**
Wayland Cres. OX11: Chil . . .4G **37**
Wayland Rd. OX12: Gro 4E **45**
Weaver Cft. OX11: Did 6A **20**
Weedon Cl. OX11: Did 3A **30**
Weedon Ct. OX10: Wal 3G **33**
Welford Gdns. OX14: Abin . . .4C **6**
Welland Av. OX11: Did 1B **30**
Welland Cl. OX13: Ship 3G **5**
Weller Cl. OX10: Ber S 1C **24**
Wellesbourne Cl.
   OX14: Abin 5D **6**
Wellshead OX11: Har 5A **28**
Wellsprings OX10: B Sot 1C **32**
Wenlock Cl. OX11: Did 1E **29**
Wensum Dr. OX11: Did 1A **30**
Wessex Rd. OX10: Ben 6F **25**
   OX11: Did 3G **29**
Wessex Way OX12: Gro 5E **45**
West Av. OX14: Abin 3C **6**
West Brook OX12: Gro 3F **45**
Westbrook Grn.
   OX11: Blew 5H **39**
Westbrook St.
   OX11: Blew 5H **39**

West Cft. OX10: Ber 1A 14
W. Down La. OX13: Marc . . .5A 4
West Dr. OX11: Har 2E 37
West End OX10: B Sot 1B 32
  OX10: Chol 4C 42
Western Av. OX11: Did 3A 30
Westfield OX11: Har 4H 27
Westfield Cl. OX10: Ben . . .5C 24
  OX12: Gro 5E 45
Westfield Rd. OX10: Ben . . .4B 24
  OX10: Chol 6B 42
  OX14: Lon W 2C 20
Westfields OX14: Abin 5H 5
Westfield Way
  OX12: Wan 2G 47
WEST HAGBOURNE 1E 39
WEST HENDRED 5A 26
West Hill OX12: Wan 3D 46
West St Helen St.
  OX14: Abin 1B 10
Westwater Way
  OX11: Did 1B 30
Wesy Quay OX14: Abin 3B 10
Weycroft OX11: Did 6A 20
Wey Rd. OX10: Ber 2B 14
Wharf Cl. OX14: Abin 1B 10
Wharf Rd. OX10: Shil 3E 23
Wharf, The OX12: Wan 2E 47
Wheatcroft Cl. OX14: Abin . . .3C 6
Wheatfields OX11: Did 4E 29
Whirlwind Way
  OX10: Ben 6F 25
Whitecross OX13: Abin 1H 5
White Hart Cl. OX10: Ben . . .5B 24

Whitehorns Farm Rd.
  OX12: Wan 2H 47
Whitehorns Way
  OX14: Dray 6E 9
White Horse Cres.
  OX12: Gro 5D 44
White Horse Leisure & Tennis Cen.
  . . . .**6E 7**
Whitehouse Cl.
  OX13: Ship 4G 5
Whiteleys Cl. OX11: Did 2H 29
Whitelock Rd. OX14: Abin . . .4B 6
White Rd. OX12: E Hen 4C 26
White's La. OX14: Rad 2F 7
Whitley Rd. OX10: Wal 5F 33
Wick Cl. OX14: Abin 3E 7
Wick Grn. OX12: Gro 3E 45
Wigod Way OX10: Wal 2G 33
Wilcher Cl. OX11: E Hag 5H 29
Wilding Rd. OX10: Wal 2F 33
WILDMOOR **4A 6**
Wildmoor Ga. OX14: Abin . . .4A 6
Willow Brook OX14: Abin . . .6H 5
Willowbrook Leisure Cen.
  . . . .**1H 29**
Willow La. OX12: Wan 4E 47
  OX14: Milt 4H 17
Willows, The OX12: Gro 6E 45
Willow Tree Cl.
  OX13: Ship 4G 5
Wills Rd. OX11: Did 2E 29
Wilmot Way OX12: Wan 1G 47
Wilsham Rd. OX14: Abin 1B 10
Wilsons Cl. OX14: Lon W 1C 20

Wimblestraw Rd.
  OX10: Ber 2A 14
Winaway OX11: Har 5H 27
Winchester Way
  OX12: Wan 2D 46
Windmill Pl. OX12: E Cha . . .3A 46
Windrush Cl. OX12: Gro 4E 45
Windrush Ct. OX14: Abin 6G 5
Windrush M. OX11: Did 6B 20
Windrush Rd. OX10: Ber . . .3A 14
Windrush Way OX14: Abin . . .4D 6
Windsor Cl. OX11: Did 3A 30
Windsor Cres.
  OX11: E Hag 5H 29
Windsor Dr. OX10: Wal 4G 33
Wingfield Cl. OX10: Ewel . . .5H 25
Winsmore La. OX14: Abin . . .1B 10
Winterborne Rd.
  OX14: Abin 6H 5
WINTERBROOK **6G 33**
Winterbrook OX10: Wal 6H 33
Winterbrook La.
  OX10: Wal 6F 33
Wintergreen La.
  OX10: Wal 6G 33
Winter's Fld. OX10: C Gif . . .4B 34
Witan Way OX12: Wan 1E 47
Withington Ct. OX14: Abin . . .6B 6
Wittenham Cl. OX10: Wal . . .2H 33
Wittenham La.
  OX10: D Tha 1B 22
Wolage Dr. OX12: Gro 6E 45
Woodcote Way *OX14: Abin* . . .3A 10
  (off Kensington Cl.)

Woodgate Cl. OX12: Gro 4E 45
Woodhill Dr. OX12: Gro 5E 45
Woodhill La. OX12: E Cha . . .4B 44
  (not continuous)
Woodlands Rd. OX11: Did . . .3E 29
Woodley Cl. OX14: Abin 2B 6
Wood's Farm Rd.
  OX12: E Hen 2A 26
Wood St. OX10: Wal 4H 33
Woodway Rd. OX11: Blew . . .6A 40
Wootton Rd. OX13: Abin 2H 5
Worcester Dr. OX11: Did 3B 30
Wordsworth Rd.
  OX14: Abin 2H 9
Wormald Rd. OX10: Wal 5G 33
Wortham Rd. OX11: Did 1F 29
Worthington Way
  OX12: Wan 1E 47
Wychwood Cl. OX10: Ben . . .5C 24
Wyndham Gdns.
  OX10: Wal 5H 33
Wyndyke Furlong
  OX14: Abin 5G 5

Y

Yare Cl. OX11: Did 1B 30
Yealm Cl. OX11: Did 5H 19
Yeld Hall Rd. OX14: Abin 3D 6
Yewtree M. OX14: Abin 6B 6
York Rd. OX11: W Hag 1E 39
Ypres Way OX14: Abin 4H 5